A Reader's Delight

A Reader's Delight

Noel Perrin

Published for Dartmouth College by
University Press of New England
Hanover and London

University Press of New England

Brandeis University	*Dartmouth College*
Brown University	*University of New Hampshire*
Clark University	*University of Rhode Island*
University of Connecticut	*Tufts University*
	University of Vermont

These articles appeared previously in the *Washington Post* in a slightly different form.

Printed in the United States of America

Library of Congress Cataloging-in-Publication Data

Perrin, Noel.
A reader's delight.

1. Books—Reviews. 2. Books and reading.
3. Bibliography—Best books. I. Title.
Z1035.A1P38 1988   028.1   87–40507
ISBN 0–87451–430–4
ISBN 0–87451–432–0 (pbk.)

5 4 3 2

Contents

Prologue vii

1. *A Nearly Perfect Comedy* 3
2. *To Awaken Quite Alone* 8
3. *A Thousand and One Chinese Nights* 14
4. *A Kind of Writing for Which No Name Exists* 20
5. *A Book That Could Cure Suicide* 25
6. *A Future Ruled by Magic* 30
7. *The Fables of George Ade* 35
8. *Falling in Love with Stendhal* 40
9. *Moving in Eccentric Circles* 46
10. *Lament for a Young Wife* 51
11. *Thinking Rabbits and Talking Crows* 57
12. *Taking Ghosts Seriously* 62
13. *The Decline and Fall of Switzerland* 68
14. *Gulliver Goes to Washington* 72
15. *Lords and Pagans* 80
16. *The Best American Novel about World War II* 84
17. *After Jane Austen, Who?* 90
18. *America's Greatest Diarist* 93
19. *The Night-and-Fog People* 100
20. *Irreverence in the Year 1239* 107
21. *A Tale of Many Virtues* 112
22. *Sailing to London* 117

23. *Men in Boxcars* 123

24. *A Man of Many Letters* 127

25. *Love, Longing, and Death* 131

26. *Philip Larkin's Greatest Poem* 136

27. *Quest of the Mulla-Mulgars* 141

28. *Prisoner in Wartime Italy* 145

29. *Ugly Ducklings and Unhappy Swans* 151

30. *In Medieval Japan* 155

31. *A Novel About Nirvana* 159

32. *In an Offhand Manner* 164

33. *Two Hundred One Years Old and Still Impudent:
The First Novel about the American
Revolution* 169

34. *Over Forty and Just Beginning:
An Englishwoman's Brilliantly Recorded Life*
173

35. *The Best of All Imaginary Islands* 177

36. *A C. S. Lewis Miscellany* 182

37. *A Girl, a Horse—and for Once a Good Book* 186

38. *A Genius Grew in Brooklyn* 190

39. *Huck Finn's French Counterpart* 194

40. *Tanya Must Die* 199

Epilogue: A Note on Availability 205

Prologue

Forgotten Books, Remembered Books
Honored Books, Orphaned Books

Since William Caxton published the first book in English in 1475, some five or ten million English-language works have appeared. Of these a few thousand are recognized classics, ranging from *The Canterbury Tales*, published by Caxton himself in 1478, up to, say, the complete poetry of Robert Frost, published in a definitive edition in 1969. They need no advertising. A few thousand more are current works of known merit. They too can look after themselves. But that leaves a large category of books just short of classic status that are known only to a handful of lucky readers. Almost anyone who reads a lot is apt to have come across at least one such book—something not in the canon, not famous, probably not even in print—but all the same sheer delight to read. Many lifelong readers have a whole collection of such books.

It's not apt to be a formal collection, like the rows and rows of Civil War books sitting on the shelves of a Civil War enthusiast, or the long line of Faulkner novels (and books of stories and poems) possessed by someone who means to own everything Faulkner ever wrote. In fact, the owner isn't likely to think of it as a collection at all. It's merely the miscellaneous group of favorite books that he or she keeps urging friends to read. All that the books have in common is that the owner thinks they are wonderful.

This volume describes my own collection, which for some years now I *have* thought of in formal terms. It is no less miscellaneous for that. There are books here by Americans, by Englishmen and women, by an Italian diplomat and a Dutch resistance fighter (who both wrote in English), by a pair of Russian brothers, by a Japanese monk. There are sixteen novels, five memoirs, four books of short stories and four of essays, a diary, a volume of letters written to an English knight, a book of animal stories, a science fiction novella, a book of fables. I think they are all wonderful.

The collection—still unconscious of itself then—got its start almost thirty years ago, back in 1960. The man who was then the librarian of Dartmouth College provided the stimulus, though he had no idea he was doing so. On occasion he would invite a senior member of the faculty to pick five favorite books and to write a paragraph about each one explaining what seemed special about it. The books then got displayed in a big glass case in the main library corridor, each with its explanatory paragraph pinned beside it. Lots of students coming down the corridor would stop and look. Colleagues generally took a peek too.

One fall day I stood looking at the five books chosen by John Wolfenden, the New Hampshire Professor of Chemistry. Mr. Wolfenden was one of the two great luminaries of the chemistry department, an Englishman whom Dartmouth had lured away from Oxford a few years earlier. I was a young instructor in the English department, and I had never even met him.

Three of his choices I have forgotten, but the other two I remember vividly. They were kids' books. *American* kids'

books. By some woman I had never heard of, named Laura
Ingalls Wilder. (This was long before *Little House* went on
television.)

It seemed wildly improbable that an English scientist would
use two of his five slots for children's books written in the
colonies, when he could have been plugging some major work
by Sir Humphrey Davy or showing off his familiarity with
Robert Boyle's *Sceptical Chemist*, that hit of the year 1661. It
made me curious. Though I wasn't even married at the time,
let alone a father with children to read aloud to, I promptly
went to the town library and checked out *Little House on the
Prairie*. I equally promptly fell in love with Mrs. Wilder's
wonderful lucid style.

Young instructors pretty much live day-to-day and can no
more imagine themselves old professors than young football
players can imagine themselves old coaches. Despite that, a
little piece of my mind raced ahead to the time when (suppos-
ing I got tenure) *I* might get invited to pick five books for the
case. I instantly knew that I would pick them Wolfenden
style—that is, not trying to impress anyone with the loftiness
of my taste or the rigor of my professionalism but merely calling attention to favorite books.

What's more, I already knew what one or two of them
would be. For example, I owned and treasured a book called
The Journal of a Disappointed Man. I had stumbled on it in a
second-hand bookstore in New York, bought it for no better
reason than that I liked the title, and then proceeded to read
it about three times, finding it more poignant each time. Nobody else I knew had ever heard of it, which gave me on the
one hand certain unattractive feelings of superiority and on
the other an authentically generous wish to share my pleasure.

Another book I could imagine putting in the case was an

obscure novel about the American Revolution. Author un-known. Title: *The Adventures of Jonathan Corncob, Loyal American Refugee.* I didn't own a copy, because the book had been out of print for about 175 years, and used copies were not something you were likely to find in a second-hand book-store. Indeed, very unlikely, since there were then only about a dozen copies in the whole United States.

I had become aware of Mr. Corncob back when I was a graduate student. I was languidly skimming a book about Tobias Smollett, the eighteenth-century English novelist, be-cause I had a paper to write and needed ideas. The book quoted a lot of eighteenth-century reviews, one of which dis-cussed not only Smollett but also this new (in 1787) novel about the American Revolution. What most caught my eye was a complaint the reviewer made. He said that *Jonathan* was quite funny but unfortunately lacked "Smollett's decency."

Smollett's decency! The Victorians didn't know he had any. If *Jonathan* was even worse, I could hardly wait to read it. After some difficulty I got hold of a copy in the library of the New York Historical Society, and did read it. Did not find it particularly obscene (though I could see right away what up-set the reviewer); did find it strikingly funny. A genuine minor masterpiece. Worthy of a spot in my display case, if I ever got to have one.

I didn't. I missed by twenty years. I had been teaching at Dartmouth for only about eighteen months and had not even advanced to assistant professor when a new librarian took over. The faculty displays ceased. I nearly forgot about them—except that when I did marry and come to have chil-dren, I certainly remembered Laura Ingalls Wilder. I had the *Little House* books ready and waiting to read before my elder daughter turned four, and I did not forget how I came to know they existed. And once in a while, when I stumbled across some minor Victorian novel such as *The Semi-Attached Couple*, read it and was enchanted, a memory surfaced. I would think of the display case and wish that it still got used for exhibiting faculty favorites.

The twenty years passed. Among all the other changes in my life, I had become an occasional book reviewer and columnist. One day I got a phone call from an editor in the Book World section of the Washington Post inviting me to write for them. The minute I got the offer, I knew exctly what I wanted to write. By now I had encountered enough neglected minor masterpicces—plus a few neglected major ones—to fill half a dozen display cases. At the moment of that phone call they shaped themselves into a collection. Everything fit. I wouldn't be limited to five. Instead of a mere paragraph I would get to write an actual article about each one. The power of a great newspaper might even help to bring a few of them back into print. (And so it has—not as often as I would wish, but three times now a book has been rescued.)

Only two rules have applied, either in writing the essays or in revising them for this volume. No book less than about fifteen years old was eligible. Younger than that it's current work, not a possible classic. And no book that more than two or three of my colleagues had read got considered. It would have been foolish to waste space on work that most people already knew.

Beyond that, anything went. If it didn't at the beginning, it came to. Originally I included only books composed in English; before I was done I had admitted four translations: two from French, one each from Russian and Japanese. How could I have omitted a book so charming as Stendahl's *On Love*, so vivid as Kenko's *Essays in Idleness?* Originally I considered only entire books; in the end I included two individual poems. Each seems to me the one absolutely great poem its author has written.

This book has no overarching pattern or grand design. Its simple purpose is to steer people toward a winter's worth or a summer's worth of unusually pleasing reading, as John Wolfenden steered me to *Little House on the Prairie*. In gratitude for which, this collection is dedicated to him.

Dartmouth College   N.P.
October 1987

A Reader's Delight

1

A Nearly Perfect Comedy

William Dean Howells was once a towering figure in American literature. The most prolific of our novelists in the late nineteenth century, he was also our leading critic. "Yours is the recognized critical Court of Last Resort in this country," Mark Twain wrote him; "from its decision there is no appeal." When he moved from Boston to New York in 1886—he was going down to become editor of *Harper's*—people said the literary capital traveled south with him. They were right. It did.

Today Howells is scarcely a name. Some people over fifty may remember suffering through *The Rise of Silas Lapham* in high school, along with that even more depressing Silas book, George Eliot's *Silas Marner*. Most people under fifty haven't read a word he wrote.

They have missed a treat. Besides his plays, his travel books, his novels of serious social uplift, Howells also wrote a dozen novels filled with sparkling comedy. One of them doesn't just sparkle—it flashes with wit, gleams with intelligence, glows with sense. That book is *Indian Summer*. It's a true minor classic.

Indian Summer is a love story, and on the surface a very romantic one. Of the three principal characters, one is a brilliant journalist of forty-one named Theodore Colville. A bachelor. Once a young student of architecture in Italy, he went home after an unhappy love affair and for the last fifteen years has been the editor of a newspaper. In what I guess to be the fall of 1882, he gets talked into running for Congress as a Democrat, is soundly defeated, and winds up going back to Italy for a long vacation.

The second is an extremely good-looking thirty-eight-year-old widow from Washington, D.C., named Lina Bowen. She knew Colville when he was young. (It was her best friend who jilted him, seventeen years ago. The two girls had been touring Europe together.) A rich woman after the death of her highly placed husband, she has gone back to Italy and settled down in a *palazzo* in Florence to give her little daughter the cultural advantages of a European upbringing.

And the third? The third is a stunningly beautiful girl of twenty named Imogene Graham. Imogene isn't just beautiful, she's also intellectual—reads constantly, longs to be valued for her mind. One of her complaints is that young men back home in Buffalo are so immature. They have no ideas, no views on life.

If Imogene were twenty in 1988 instead of in 1882, she would probably be something like a Vassar student on her junior year abroad with plans later to join the Peace Corps. As it is, she has talked her family into letting her spend the winter in Florence under the chaperonage of her mother's old friend Lina Bowen.

Since the American community in Florence is both small and stable—the time of the two-week tourist is still in the remote future—Colville runs into Mrs. Bowen almost as soon as he arrives in the city. She had been ready to like him back when they were young, something he never noticed then but has realized in retrospect, and she is happy to see him again now. The discreet beginnings of a romance occur. Lucky Colville!

That's not the half of his luck, though. Imogene is equally

attracted. Partly it's that she has never met such an interesting man before, let alone one so witty. Partly it's that her romantic nature thrills to the (erroneous) idea that he has been living with a broken heart all these years and that she can make it up to him.

As for Colville, he is profoundly attached to both women (he even likes the little daughter), and before the book is many chapters old, he is half in love with both. But he can, of course, marry only one.

Such choices are hardly rare in fiction—on the contrary, they are the staple of cheap romance. You can buy books with plots like this by the hundreds at any airport. In fact, it's hard to buy anything else.

But Howells was the man who introduced realism to American fiction. In *Indian Summer* he has done that rare thing: he has written a realistic romantic comedy. The down-to-earthness and the good sense don't destroy the romance, they deepen it.

Realism touches *Indian Summer* in many ways. The central one is through Colville's own awareness. The story is told from his point of view—and his point of view is the complex, wry, tender, sensible one of a clever middle-aged man. Even when he is most drawn to beautiful young Imogene, he is aware that she is much stronger in enthusiasm than in judgment. *She* is trapped almost wholly in the present—she can't really imagine old people ever having been so young, or young ones as they will be when old. *He* can easily range back and forth—foreseeing what Imogene will be like at thirty-eight (delightful), remembering what he himself was like at twenty, and so on. He has double awareness to her single, and that double awareness figures in the book like a person playing the piano with two hands instead of one.

Besides that, there are two shrewd observers in the book,

each a marvelous creation. One is a retired New England clergyman, the Reverend Mr. Waters, who has come to spend his old age in Florence. He may be modeled a little on Emerson. In any event, he is a wonderfully detached and acute observer of human life. His many conversations with Colville include some of the best dialogue ever written in an American novel.

The other is an old lady named Mrs. Amsden, a woman who was a beauty in youth and who has been a charmer and an eager gossip at all ages. She is as frivolous as Mr. Waters is deep, but she's also smart.

Like all the other Americans in Florence, she is fascinated by the Colville-Bowen-Graham triangle, and she speculates freely on how it's going to turn out. "He is a bachelor," she tells an enthralled friend early on, "and there is a natural affinity between bachelors and widows—much more than if he were a widower, too. If he were a widower, I should say it was undoubtedly mademoiselle. If he were a little *bit* younger, I should have no doubt it was madame; but men of that age have such an ambition to marry young girls! . . . If he were wise—which he probably isn't, if he's like other men in such matters—there wouldn't be any question about Mrs. Bowen. Pretty creature! And so much sense! Too much for him. Ah, my dear, how we are wasted upon that sex!"

That speech pretty well captures the spirit of the book: affectionate, clever, clear-eyed—and full of praise for women. In one sense, the book is Howells's tribute to the wonder of women at all ages, from little Effie, who is about nine, to Mrs. Amsden who must be near eighty. She's still fond of flirting, despite her total loss of looks, and Howells says of her in his own voice, "One realizes in looking at such old ladies that there are women who could manage their own skeletons winningly." No illusions there but much affection and a happy phrase. So with the whole book.

But I should quite stalling. Who *does* Colville marry? If you're a clever observer, you already know. And if not, well, that's one more incentive to read a very pleasureable book.

Indian Summer.
William Dean Howells. 1886.

2

To Awaken Quite Alone

For two hundred years a whole class of clever, talented, and utterly intrepid Englishwomen have been traveling to the most dangerous parts of the world. Lady Hester Stanhope, who left England in 1810, and eventually settled in an abandoned convent in what was then a remote part of the Ottoman Empire and is now Lebanon, was a model of the type.

Lady Hester came of a political family, and in youth she found London reasonably amusing, what with Parliament and all. This was especially true of the period in her twenties when she served both as official hostess and as private secretary to one of her uncles, who chanced to be the prime minister. But William Pitt died when she was twenty-nine, and then mere social life began to pall. Soon she went off to one of the remoter parts of Wales, in search of adventure. When Wales proved too tame, she sailed for Gibraltar and eventually the Ottoman Empire. By 1815 she had a *firman* from the sultan himself, giving her quite a lot of authority with the pashas of Acre and Damascus, an authority she used with great freedom. If you want to know more, look at the biography by her niece, the Duchess of Cleveland.

Freya Stark joined the procession of intrepid woman travelers somewhat over a century later. She came of a family quite as eccentric as Lady Hester's, though less socially grand. After learning Arabic and then Persian, Miss Stark began in the late 1920s to make trips to what were still very wild places indeed. Some of them, like Yemen and the Hadhramaut, are not entirely tame even now.

She had many purposes: to explore places where few or no other Europeans had ever been; to find historic sites such as the old battlegrounds of Alexander the Great; to make maps; to look for hidden treasures of various kinds; to climb mountains like Takht-i-Suleiman, the Throne of Solomon. Most of all, though, she wanted to lead the life of the country and to be in the middle of whatever danger or excitement there was to be in the middle of. She generally was.

Starting in 1934, she began to write a series of wonderful books about these trips. There are few travel books better than *The Southern Gates of Arabia* or *The Valleys of the Assassins* or *A Winter in Arabia*. Only, "travel book" is too cozy and safe a name—these are books composed equally of adventure and of fine observation.

There was much to observe. Miss Stark was present in many places at the very last moment before ancient cultures gave way to cars and planes and radios, and this was no accident. Back in 1921, when a very great professor, a family friend, was urging her to learn Icelandic (so as to read the sagas), she chose Arabic instead. She foresaw the changes oil drilling was likely to bring to the whole Middle East, and she wanted to watch them happen: "I thought the most interesting things in the world were likely to happen in the neighborhood of oil." Even then, as a very young woman, she knew she wanted to take part in current sagas more than she wanted to read old ones.

Of all her books, my favorite is *The Valleys of the Assassins*. It's an account of five different trips she took to Iran between 1930 and 1932. It takes its title from the two of those trips she devoted to exploring the sites of Assassin castles, of which Iran was once full. The Assassins were a heretical branch of the Isma'ili sect of Muslims, very warlike. In the twelfth and thirteenth centuries they had a chain of fifty-some castles across Persia. Nearly all of them were destroyed by Tatar invaders in the year 1256—which didn't keep Freya Stark from rediscovering some of their sites in 1931. Among other things, she is a good if amateur archeologist and a highly professional geographer.

But it's neither for archeology nor for geography that I love *The Valleys of the Assassins*. It's for the details of the journeys, and for the character of Freya Stark herself.

Take the first trip, which was into Luristan in 1931. That Iranian province is now full of oil wells and technicians and modern debris. In 1931, the first motor road was just being built by order of the shah but not yet in use. Ponies, donkeys, and black oxen were the transport; the newly introduced police made their occasional patrols on fast horses. The nomad Lurs were building houses, also by order of the shah, but not living in them. They preferred their tents and their freedom to follow the flocks to summer and winter pasture, just as they preferred their Lurish dress and hairstyle to the modern style the shah intended to force on them.

Freya Stark was there primarily to rob graves, but she also got to see the very last moment of pure Lurish life. A typical night would be the one she spent in the village of Beira, sleeping (with many other people) in the headman's tent. This structure in no way resembled what Boy Scouts use. "One side was open: a long line of black oxen with felt rugs on their backs blocked it and acted as a wind-screen: they chewed their feed gently through the night, while we slept as well as we could with rivulets of cold air creeping down our spines: now and then some tribesman, pirate-faced in the half-darkness, would rouse himself, heap an armful of thorns on the embers, and fill the tent with strange shadows and a fleeting warmth."

The next day she moves on to the valley of Gatchenah, "lined from end to end with graveyards of every date and description," and settles down to buy bronzes from the graves and to offer a reward to any Lur who can find her a complete prehistoric skull. All this was, of course, illegal, and Freya Stark tended to be in trouble with the police just as much as the Lurs themselves, which was one of the bonds between them. But before anyone concludes it was also *wrong*, I should mention that pre-Islamic relics tend to be roughly handled in Muslim countries. The shah's new road incorporated untold thousands of pagan gravestones as fill; one very early mountain castle she visited had had surviving rooms until just a few years before when an unusually daring tribesman had climbed up to examine it. Then he demolished everything he could "as having belonged to the infidels." Freya Stark can be regarded as preserver as much as thief. She got her skull, incidentally, and it is right now in a museum in Baghdad.

Or take the second trip, which was a literal treasure hunt. A young Lurish exile in Baghdad came to her with a map. It had been made by a tribesman of his father's, who had found a cave "with twenty cases of gold ornaments, daggers, coins, and idols" and brought his chief as much as he could conceal in his clothing for proof. Freya and the young man are to find the cave, and get it all; that is, provided they can avoid both the police and the other person who knows about the treasure, an ex-vizier in Mosul, a man of power, quite prepared to imprison and even to murder anyone who stands in his way.

The story is too complicated to tell here, but it is very much worth reading in *The Valleys of the Assassins*. There is ploy and counterploy, plot and counterplot, all of it done in the high style of Persian courtesy. Some of Freya's devices for throwing the police off the trail would hold the respectful attention of James Bond. Hers have the advantage of having really happened.

If these adventures (and there are dozens I have no room to mention) are half of what makes the book enchanting, the other half is the author herself. First-person narratives are tricky, and trickiest of all when the author is a brilliant person doing brilliant things. Either he winds up sounding boastful, or he stuffs in a lot of mock modesty and self-deprecation.

Freya Stark does neither, yet she comes out utterly sympathetic. Partly that's because she is so good a reporter that she can report her own doings in the same detached way she tells anyone's story. Partly it's the humor with which the book gleams. Partly it's that she's a woman, traveling alone in places where custom and law give so many advantages to men that any gain she scores one can't help cheering for. Partly it's the complete absence in her of mean emotions like envy. One example: She herself is quite plain, and has minded being so. In a volume of autobiography called *The Coast of Incense*, she once wrote, "The want of a regular education has never caused me any regret, but the absence of beauty has always been disappointing; I have managed without it, but even now [she was sixty when she wrote this] I cannot help thinking how much more fun to myself and others I might have procured, but for the absence of a few pigments, a millimeter here or there, a tiny tilt of chin or eyebrow, which those who possess them often scarcely know how to manipulate, and which I felt I might have animated to very great advantage." Nevertheless, she delights openly in the many forms that good looks take in different Kurdish or Lurish or Arab tribes, and never fails to mention a pretty wife or daughter. Unlike male travelers, of course, she sees them unveiled.

But most of all, it's because one is in the presence of a truly adventurous spirit. The reader can't help being roused— and becoming a little more alive. In *Baghdad Sketches*, Freya Stark writes, "To awaken quite alone in a strange town is one of the pleasantest sensations in the world." And in *A Winter in Arabia*, standing on a mountain ridge, looking down on the fortified oasis of Yeb'eth and the caravan routes beyond, she writes, "To travel from fortress to fortress, over the high jol, where men still walk with guns upon their shoulders, and at the end of days to see before you land that is yet unknown— what enchantment in this world, I should like to know, is comparable to this?"

The Valleys of the Assassins.
Freya Stark. 1934.

3

A Thousand and One Chinese Nights

Which writers of English have the most complicated, artificial, and generally improbable styles? The mannerists, of course. If you put someone like Hemingway, with his aversion to adjectives and love of short sentences, at one end of the spectrum, you would put mannerists at the other. They employ adjectives and adverbs as freely as a maker of birthday cakes employs festoons of icing and small candles, while their sentence structure tends toward the baroque and even the rococo.

Mannerists have been around for some centuries. As long ago as 1578, John Lyly published the story of the young traveler Euphues, his friend Philautus, and the beautiful Camilla. Camilla was the best-looking woman in Naples (which in 1578 was the largest city in Europe). Here is part of how Lyly conveys that information: "For as the finest Ruby staineth the color of the rest that be in place, or as the Sun dimmeth the Moon, that she cannot be discerned, so this gallant girl, more fair than fortunate, and yet more fortunate than faithful, eclipsed the beauty of them all, and changed their colors." There are two metaphors, three alliterations, five adjectives, and eight compositional elements in that sentence, and it's not even one of the longer ones.

Lyly had a huge success—enough so that it amused Shakespeare to parody him (Falstaff does a funny imitation of eu-

phuism in *Henry IV*), but no one would now read him for pleasure. The case is quite different with the mannerists who
flourished at the end of the nineteenth and the beginning of
the twentieth centuries. People still crowd in to see *The Im-
portance of Being Earnest*, that very mannered play by Oscar
Wilde. Sir Max Beerbohm's *Zuleika Dobson* continues to give
pleasure to many, and there are even those (I am one of them)
who hug themselves with delight at the novels of Ronald
Firbank. How can one not like an author who writes sentences such as this one from *Valmouth*? Captain Thorough-
fare of the Royal Navy is explaining to his fiancée why he has
brought a young sailor from his ship home on leave with him.
It's an explanation any gay person would understand at once.
"That little lad, upon a cruise, is, to me, what Patroclus was
to Achilles, and even more." What timing! What splendor of
commas!

Ernest Bramah was contemporary with Beerbohm and
Firbank and considerably more mannered than either of
them. Though himself of the plainest possible background—
his real name was Ernest Smith, and he was born in Man-
chester, England, of quite ordinary parents—he spent most
of his life writing what can only be described as the Chinese
equivalent of the Arabian Nights.

It came about like this. In early manhood Bramah encountered the highly ritualized and super-polite mode of speech
employed by well-bred Chinese before the revolution. It involved careful avoidance of ego display (one said "this person," not "I"), elaborate compliments to the person one was
addressing, insincere insults to oneself, and as much circum-
locution as possible. All this enchanted Bramah, and he
rapidly began to develop an English version, a sort of Anglo-
Mandarin speech, which is both extremely comic ("gravity re-

ducing" you'd say in Anglo-Mandarin) and as supple as a well-made glove. It was then his inspiration to invent the quick-witted and endlessly resourceful story-teller Kai Lung and enlist him as narrator. Kai Lung plays the role that Scheherazade does in the Arabian Nights.

In the end, Bramah wrote five books of Kai Lung stories and published them at leisurely intervals between 1900 and 1940. All are worth reading, providing one likes artifice. But the one likeliest to be greeted with actual cries of delight is *Kai Lung's Golden Hours*, which first began to reduce gravity in 1922.

As the book opens, Kai Lung is on his way by foot from Loo-chow to the city of Yu-ping, where he hopes to earn a few taels telling stories in the marketplace. At noon he stops to take a nap in a small wood. He is woken by the sound of girlish laughter: two young women have noticed his sleeping form and are standing some distance away under a wild fig tree. He gets up, bowing politely. "At this display the elder and less attractive of the two maidens fled, uttering loud and continuous cries of apprehension in order to conceal the direction of her flight."

Kai Lung barely notices her departure because he is so entranced by the other maiden. They are soon deep in conversation. Having learned that he is a professional teller of stories, she plies him with questions. Among them, she is curious to learn what kind of story pays best, or as she delicately puts it, which is the kind "whereby your collecting bowl is the least ignored?"

"'That depends on the nature and condition of those who stand around, and therein lies much that is essential to the art,' replied Kai Lung, not without an element of pride.

'Should the company be chiefly formed of the illiterate and

the immature of both sexes, stories depicting the embarrass-
ment of unnaturally round-bodied mandarins, the unpremedi-
tated flight of eccentrically-garbed passers-by into vats of
powdered rice, the despair of guardians of the street [we call
them policemen] when assaulted by showers of eggs and over-
ripe lo-quats, or any other variety of humiliating pain in-
flicted upon the innocent and unwary, never fail to win approval. The prosperous and substantial find contentment in
hearing of the unassuming virtues and frugal lives of the poor
and unsuccessful. Those of humble origin, especially tea-
house maidens and the like, are only really at home among
stories of the exalted and quick-moving, the profusion of their
robes, the magnificence of their palaces, and the general
high-minded depravity of their lives.'"

If you find some similarity here to the preferred reading of
various groups of English people and Americans, it is no accident. Bramah loved to describe home matters under the
elaborate Chinese disguise. I am quite clear, for example,
that he was taking a polished revenge on some actual English
barber when he has Kai Lung tell the story of Chou-hu, the
Peking pigtail embellisher who habitually engages his cus-
tomers "in diffuse and refined conversation."

Meanwhile, things are progressing in the wood. In due
course, the maiden asks Kai Lung to tell *her* a story, and he
instantly proposes the one about Princess Taik and the min-
strel Ch'eng.

"'Is it,' inquired the maiden, with an agreeable glance to
ward the opportune recumbence of a fallen tree, 'is it a narra-
tion that would lie within the passage of the sun from one
branch of this willow to another?'

'Adequately set forth, the history of the Princess Taik and
of the virtuous youth occupies all the energies of an agile

story-teller for seven weeks,' replied Kai Lung, not entirely gladdened that she should deem him capable of offering so meager an entertainment as that she indicated."

At this point there is a dramatic interruption, and poor Kai Lung never gets to tell the story at all. When he next meets the maiden, he is a prisoner in Yu-ping, momentarily awaiting execution at the hands of the evil mandarin Shan Tien, and she is the favored fair one of the mandarin's inner chamber. (It was in attempting to escape this fate that she had come to the wood.) Her name, he now learns, is Hwa-mei.

From here on, the plot of the book is as simple as the style is complex. Egged on by his malicious secretary, the mandarin keeps resolving to put Kai Lung to high-minded torture, and then kill him. Kai Lung's ability to tell stories that are apt to Shan Tien's own circumstances, and even more Hwa-mei's brilliant stratagems, keep delaying it. At the end, both of them win free and go out to eat their rice together.

Meanwhile, Kai Lung has told ten absolutely glorious stories. (Nine to the mandarin, and one specially for the girl after they have escaped.) He has told the story of Ning, the captive god; the story of Hien, the virtuous youth who has failed the literary examinations eleven times running, and of his arch-rival Tsin Lung, who earns much silver helping people cheat on those same examinations; the story of the young heiress Fa Fei, "whose mind was so liberally stored with graceful accomplishments as to give rise to the saying that to be in her presence was more refreshing than to sit in a garden of perfumes listening to the wisdom of seven elderly philosophers." And many others as good.

This degraded and incapable reviewer doubtless errs through his very discreditable lack of training in contemporary Chinese thought. He nevertheless ventures to assert that reading Mr. Bramah will yield more pleasure than twenty solemn books about politics and industry in the emerging Orient.

Kai Lung's Golden Hours.
Ernest Bramah. 1922.

4

A Kind of Writing for Which No Name Exists

Just offhand, I can name four major American writers, each alive and healthy, who for one reason or another do not currently publish. They haven't for decades. They write, but they don't publish.

J. D. Salinger is, of course, the best known. No book from him since *Raise High the Roof-Beam, Carpenters* in 1963. Then there is Ralph Ellison. *Invisible Man* came out in 1952, and there has been nothing since except a book of essays— and even that was twenty years ago. Next comes Walter M. Miller. *A Canticle for Leibowitz* appeared in 1960 (Miller was thirty-seven at the time), and it has gradually come to be acknowledged as one of the half-dozen best works of science fiction ever written. What has Miller published in the ensuing quarter of a century? One volume of short stories: old ones. All of them first appeared in magazines in the 1950s.

Finally, there is Joseph Mitchell. *His* last book appeared in 1965.

The first three at least allow their books to stay in print, so that book stores stock them, and people who grew up in the 1970s and 80s find them and read them. Mitchell doesn't even permit that. The result is that Salinger and Ellison con-

tinue to be famous, and if Miller's name is not instantly recognizable, the title of his masterpiece is. But Joseph Mitchell
is barely known to people under forty-five. People under
forty-five are missing a treat.

Mitchell is a North Carolinian who became a New Yorker.
He went straight from the University of North Carolina to a
New York newspaper. First a reporter, he quickly turned into
a feature writer, and then he became an essayist, the best in
the city. Some think he was (and is) the best in the country.
Others, more temperate, put him in a tie for first with John
McPhee.

Before he ceased to publish, Mitchell brought out five
books. At least two of them are masterpieces: *McSorley's
Wonderful Saloon* and *The Bottom of the Harbor*. I love both,
but I love *The Bottom of the Harbor* more. I've reread it every
three or four years for twenty-five years, and my opinion of it
is still climbing.

The book contains six long essays, all connected with the
waterfront. One—the only one some lesser person might have
written—is about rats: the three varieties that inhabit New
York, spread plagues, come and go on ships. That piece is
merely brilliant reporting.

The other five are a kind of writing for which there is no
name. Each tells a story, and is dramatic; each is both wildly
funny and so sad you can hardly bear it; each tells its story so
much in the words of its characters that it feels like a kind of
apotheosis of oral history. Finally, like the Icelandic sagas,
each combines a fierce joy in the physicality of living with a
stoical awareness that all things physical end in death, usually preceded by years of diminishment. One winds up admir-
ing Mitchell's characters (all real people), loving them, all
but weeping for them, maybe hoping to live as gallantly.

Take the piece called "The Rivermen." It begins with
Mitchell describing the Hudson River and his own habit of
going over to the New Jersey shore to watch it, since the Manhattan shore is largely inaccessible. He used to do his watching in the railroad yards in Jersey City and Weehawken. Ignoring all the No Trespassing signs, he'd sneak out to the end
of a railroad pier and sit gazing at the river. There's endless
traffic of tugs and barges and ships. Once there was something else: a six-foot sturgeon, right there in the shipping
lanes. "It rose twice, and cleared the water both times, and I
plainly saw its bristly snout and its shiny little eyes and its
white belly and its glistening, greenish-yellow, bony-plated,
crocodilian back and sides, and it was a spooky sight."

Eventually every single railroad policeman on the shore
became aware of him, and then he had to move on. At this
point he discovers the town of Edgewater, New Jersey, which
is to New York City rather as the sturgeon is to the shipping in
the harbor. It's also where the rivermen he is going to write
about live.

Edgewater is across from upper Manhattan, between 94th
and 164th Streets. It's a town of maybe four thousand people,
strung out along a narrow plain at the foot of the Palisades. It
was settled in the 1630s by Dutch and French Huguenot
farmers; their descendants are living in Edgewater still. Half
the people in town are related.

Edgewater is a wonderful place to watch the river from.
The natives have been watching the Hudson, and fishing in
it, and running boats on it for three and a half centuries, and
Mitchell fits right in. He soon gets to know some of the
middle-aged and old men who own barges (former railroad
barges), which they keep just offshore and which they use in
the spring for shad fishing. They use them all year round for
clubhouses.

The heart of the piece is the story that old Harry Lyons tells, sitting on his barge one February afternoon. He's not telling it to Mitchell but to a man his own age named Townsend, the brother-in-law of another Edgewater man who has brought him by to show him what a shad barge is like.

The story is about the shad fishing that old Harry is still doing, very vigorous fishing, using pole nets twelve hundred feet long, sometimes catching a thousand shad in one haul. It's also about the whole past of shad fishing and of the Hudson and of Edgewater and of Harry himself. It's also about youth and old age. And it's about good eating, especially shad roe and oysters. And most of all it's about the incredible survival of Edgewater right next to Manhattan. Mitchell, who has a genius for finding real-life metaphors, tells you early on about an old graveyard in the lower part of the town. It's quite a large one, and it's still in use. It is entirely surrounded, however, by a modern factory—a huge one, belonging to the Aluminum Company of America. The cemetery forms a two-acre garden in the middle. Funerals go in and out through the factory gate, as do people visiting graves or people who simply want to picnic in the beautiful old graveyard. That was part of the agreement when the company bought part of what was once the Vreeland farm.

Not only that, there are rosebushes in there, descended from a rosebush that came from Holland in the 1630s. Or so, at least, Mitchell hears from an old woman whom he meets (and naturally gets to know) while she is gardening in the graveyard.

Mitchell himself could be called a gardener in a graveyard, if that didn't make him sound much more lugubrious and much less fun to read than he actually is. In another piece called "Up in the Old Hotel," he tells a story about Louis Moreno, the owner of a restaurant near the Fulton Fish Mar-

ket, and about the old, old six-story brick building the restaurant is in, and about a visit he and Louie make to the four
long-unused upper stories. To read it is to time-travel back
not only through the long history of New York City but almost
clear back to New Amsterdam. The critic Stanley Edgar
Hyman was so moved by the account of that trip to the upper
floors with their boarded windows and heaps of dust that he
once wrote a full-scale Freudian interpretation of it. I don't
know that I find Hyman's interpretation fully convincing.
I do know that Mitchell has the gift of making roses bloom in
the darkest and most unexpected places.

The Bottom of the Harbor.
Joseph Mitchell. 1960.

5

A Book That Could Cure Suicide

The year is 1903. A thirteen-year-old boy in a little English town has started keeping a journal. At first it's practically all science. "Am writing an essay on the life-history of insects, and have abandoned the idea of writing on 'How Cats Spend Their Time,'" he notes. Later that year he takes a sort of vow to learn all about beetles.

The boy's name is Bruce Cummings, and he comes from a background as drab as his name. His father works for an obscure provincial newspaper, making just enough money to count as middle class. Nobody in that family goes to college. Everybody in it starts work young.

Bruce picked the wrong family to be born in. What *he* wants is first education—lots and lots of it, at the best schools—and then fame. He'd like to be a great biologist, preferably the greatest of his generation.

He knows he has the temperament. By the time he's fifteen, he is reading Darwin, dissecting leeches, teaching himself chemistry. At sixteen, when he catches measles, he can look at his own body with a calm scientific eye and note, "I have somewhere near 10,000 spots on me." He can look at his mind (he loves to do this—he is self-intoxicated) and suspect himself of genius. And all the time he is pouring thoughts into his journal. What he doesn't know yet is that he is an extraordinarily good writer.

But the English class system does not easily let go of people. Eighty years ago, it hardly let go at all.

At barely seventeen, Bruce Cummings left school forever, and reluctantly signed what he called his Death Warrant—a five-year bond of apprenticeship on his father's paper. Six days a week for five years he must labor at what doesn't interest him. Being stubborn, he continued studying biology, physics, chemistry and German in the evenings, and dissecting owls and frogs on Sundays. But he was trapped, and he knew it.

There was one escape route. The British government supported a tiny handful of scientific institutions. Staff jobs in them were filled by competitive examination. Win the exam, and you got the job. Unfortunately for the self-educated, such exams were not open to just anybody. You had to be invited to take them. Ordinarily, smart young graduates of Oxford, Cambridge, and London got invited, having been nominated by their professors. No others need apply. But if a Devonshire apprentice could get nominated, he did have a right to sit the exam.

The year he was twenty-one, Cummings managed to get a nomination. Three places were open in the British Museum of Natural History. He did pretty well for someone with no academic training—he came in fourth.

The next year he did even better. There was another competition. Two jobs open. A roomful of eager university graduates, plus Bruce Cummings, were there to take the exam.

He placed first by a wide margin. And so at twenty-two he vaulted up in the social structure, moved to London, and became a scientist. "I'm in, in, in!" he writes in his journal. Soon his keen provincial eye is noting all the wonders of London. He begins to publish in magazines like *The Journal of*

Botany and *Science Progress*. He discovers Beethoven, and goes in ecstasy to hear Sir Henry Wood conduct the Fifth. It's hard for someone in the radio-TV-VCR age even to imagine the wonder of that evening. He drops his drab provincial name, and flames out as W. N. P. Barbellion. (The whole name is charged with significance. Besides its pleasing foreignness, Barbellion combines "barbarian" and "rebellion." As for three initials, they were and still are a class indicator in England—they indicate gentry. The three names Barbellion hid behind those chaste initials . . . well, you'll see later.)

This is a delightful success story, made still more delightful by the fact that Barbellion was such a lively man. Many scientists are brilliant, single-focused, and boring. Barbellion was brilliant, multi-focused, and fascinating. From age sixteen on, his journal gradually expanded to include all the things that interested him.

For example, there were girls. Barbellion adored girls, both in the reverent Victorian fashion, and in every other fashion you can think of. He even adored them scientifically. Once in Devonshire he spent an evening with a girl named Mary, and achieved a modest degree of intimacy. Afterwards he wrote in his journal, "I hope to goodness she doesn't think I want to marry her. In the Park in the dark, kissing her. I was testing and experimenting with a new experience."

In London, he sits behind an Irish girl (and her date) in a theater. "She was dark, with shining blue eyes, and a delightful little nose of the utmost import to every male who should gaze upon her." They manage to exchange smiles—twice— and all night he can think of nothing else. Two days later a newspaper is indignantly refusing to run his ad trying to get in touch with her; they suspect he's recruiting prostitutes.

When he later gets engaged to Eleanor Benger, a young artist he truly reveres, he can be surprised to find that in the middle of what he calls a "devotional" embrace, a part of his mind is thinking, "Hot stuff, this witch." Few Englishmen allowed such thoughts to surface then, much less rushed home to record them in a diary.

If Barbellion had lived to be a Fellow of the Royal Society, an old professor with a knighthood, as he dreamed of doing, his journal would still be among the twenty or so best in English. Right up there with Thoreau, Pepys, and George Templeton Strong. But Barbellion didn't live. His knowledge that he wouldn't is what gives the journal its greatest poignancy. I have saved one aspect of his story until now. It is this aspect that led Barbellion to call his book *The Journal of a Disappointed Man.*

Back when he was twenty, still in Barnstaple, he got handed a second death warrant—and this was no metaphor for a disagreeable job, but a warrant in earnest. He had a terrible heart attack, and the doctor who saw him discovered that he'd been born with an incurable disease. He could expect to die at any time. Worse yet, if by chance he did live a while, he could expect to see his health gradually deteriorate. (He got his first slight partial paralysis at twenty-three, the same year that the sight of one eye was affected.)

From then until he actually did die, just after his thirtieth birthday, Barbellion reckoned his future in months, or at most single years. "I badly want to live say another twelve months," he wrote at age twenty-four, at a time when he was first deeply in love and first beginning to publish widely. It was not to be counted on.

Another man might have gone into depression, especially as the paralysis grew on him. Certainly Barbellion had his dark hours. And it is in that sense that this is the journal of a disappointed man.

But being who he was, he mostly responded by trying to cram fifty years of life into the little time he had. To an astonishing degree he succeeded. He did marry Eleanor (she knowing exactly what she was getting into) and even had a child. He saw and embraced the whole life of his time. If he and Eleanor are staying on a farm, sitting together in a flowery glade exchanging kisses, he can still use his good eye to notice one of the farm hens wandering by in search of bugs and think from its point of view. "How nice to be a chicken in a field of Buttercups and see them as big as Sunflowers!" Or himself wandering through London, he can soar up and look at his fellow men and women from the heights—look in love, scorn, pity, and finally admiration, overcome with the drama of practically all lives, tender with the desire that all should be recorded, as in some great never-ending film of the cosmos. "If there be no loving God to watch us, it's a pity for His sake as much as for our own."

This journal is one of the great affirmations in our literature. If I had a friend who found life tedious, who was maybe even suicidal, and I had the power to make him or her read one book, it would be the soul-stirring diary of Wilhelm Nero Pilate Barbellion, alias plain Bruce Cummings.

The Journal of a Disappointed Man.
W. N. P. Barbellion. 1919.

6

A Future Ruled by Magic

Experts—all kinds of experts—love to gaze into the future. Having gazed, they love to tell the rest of us what they see coming. As the writer William Tucker once noted, there is "a whole cottage industry" staffed by experts with telescopes. The industry's product: "computer print-outs and two-volume studies, all continuously spewing out information telling us what the world is going to be like in the year 2020." One thing that nearly all these future worlds have in common is that they are depressing. Very scientific and very depressing.

It is not inevitable that imagined futures be dreary, however. Suppose that instead of a team of economists or the world's six leading demographers, a poet did the gazing. Suppose that poet was a well-known wit, and as much at home in prose as in poetry. Suppose him an enemy of the bureaucratic state.

But no need to suppose—this work exists. It is Robert Graves's glorious novel *Watch the North Wind Rise*. It presents one of the oddest and most delightful futures I know. At times I can persuade myself that something like it might really happen.

The book opens around a thousand years from now in a little kingdom in what is now southern France. A poet from our own era named Edward Venn-Thomas has been summoned into the future. It is he who tells the story. As the book

30

begins, he is just rubbing his eyes, and coming to, in a house inhabited by the five magicians who summoned him. They are waiting in the next room while an interpreter who speaks English of the late Christian period (that's us) helps him get his bearings.

The first thing Venn-Thomas notices is a wood fire, and that surprises him. "Prophets of my epoch," he says to the interpreter, "have promised a future in which atomic energy will supersede wood, coal, and electricity in domestic heating."

"That was a very temporary future and, according to the *Brief History*, not at all a happy one. Would you care for a drink?"

Venn-Thomas would love one, and the interpreter brings him a glass of beer and a plate of pretzels. Both the glass and the plate are beautiful hand work, and Venn-Thomas asks if they are valuable.

This question baffles the interpreter. Finally he says, "If you mean: 'are they valued as worthy of daily use?' the answer is, that we use no objects that are not so valued."

No, no, answers Venn-Thomas impatiently. "What I meant was: do they cost a lot of money?"

"Money? Money went out of use long, long ago. It misbehaved, you see." (And so did credit cards, electronic transfer of funds, etc., all of which have also gone out of use.)

It's already obvious that this future is different from any that a team of bank presidents would foresee. It becomes even more obvious when the interpreter takes Venn-Thomas into the next room to meet the five magicians. One is a witch—a quite beautiful witch in her early thirties—named Leaf-of-the-Sallow. She is still dressed for the evocation: conical moleskin hat, long embroidered robe, bare feet painted blue. Another is a nymph (literal sense) of about twenty called Sapphire. The other three are men: poet-wizards. Together they form the complement of magicians in the village of Horned Lamb. Like every other village, it is divided into five estates: captains, recorders (the interpreter is of this estate), commons, magicians, and servants, corresponding to the five fingers of the hand.

In addition to falling instantly in love with Sapphire, Venn-Thomas now begins to get from the magicians a systematic account of the world he is in. Things have changed a lot.

Just for starters, Christianity and all other male-dominated religions have vanished utterly. Humanity worships The Goddess, one of whose names is Mari. High technology has also vanished, with many interesting results. For example, not only are there no computers spewing data out, there isn't even printing. This is the result of a conscious decision to keep the quantity of stored knowledge within the grasp of a human mind. What about the poet-magicians of Horned Lamb, you wonder. How do they publish? Answer: any poet, on coming of age, is given twenty small silver plates on which he or she may have poems engraved. That's the life supply. It tends to make writers quite selective about what they choose to print.

Clocks have also been abolished. ("Since Time is money, / Time must be destroyed," that great future poet Vives wrote.) One of my favorite details in the book describes the way in which school starts in the morning. It can hardly begin on the dot of 8:30. Instead what happens in each village is that sooner or later children begin to drift over to the schoolhouse. When the third child arrives, he or she rings the bell. Then the teacher and the other children set out, and the school day begins.

What has replaced time, money, and machinery is ritual, handicraft, and love. This is a world a little like the Middle

Ages, in that everything is intensely local, personal, and shining in bright clear colors. But mainly it is a world like no other at all.

Venn-Thomas learns from the magicians how the world came into being. What happened was that sometime around 2020, or maybe it was 2200, science achieved full control of our planet. Government became totally rational, and world wide. War ceased; religion withered away to scattered sects; the doctrine called Economic Logicalism ruled supreme.

At that point a disease called colabromania began to strike the best, coldest, and most rational thinkers. It took this form: they began to whirl like dervishes, foam at the mouth, and commit acts of insane violence. This is the work of Mari. She has decided that male logic, fomented by Zeus, Jehovah, Allah, etc., has had a long enough run, and that it is time to restore rule by feminine impulse and insight.

People in 2020 or whenever don't know that; they just know that the best scientists are all going nuts (they have to be "lethalized") and that government is breaking down. An Israeli anthropologist named ben-Yeshu comes to the rescue. He concludes that mankind took a wrong turn somewhere in the remote past, and that experiments are needed to find out where. He persuades the world council to set up enclaves: a Stone Age culture, Bronze Age, and so on. One of these enclaves comprises the island of Crete, and it reproduces Minoan culture (as Graves imagines it), complete with worship of the Mother Goddess. That turns out to have been a good idea. Within a century or two, New Cretan ideas are dominant in most of the world, and it is to one of the many small New Cretan kingdoms that Venn-Thomas gets summoned. War, incidentally, makes a vigorous reappearance in New Cretan culture, with all sorts of splendid fighting—but hardly any casualties. The fighting is with quarterstaves. One of the best sections in the book narrates the war between the polyandrous village of Rabnon and the monogamous village of Zapmor, fought from dawn to dark on a Tuesday. (All wars are fought on Tuesdays.) The two-village feast afterward makes quite a scene too.

Watch the North Wind Rise is a book so rich in style and plot, so profoundly mythic and at the same time so lightly comic, not to mention so full of twists, turns, and trick reversals, that there is simply no way to communicate its full flavor. I won't even try. Perhaps the best I can do is to report that when I first read it, I spent many a night all but literally praying to Mari that the next time the magicians of New Crete evoke a few people from our century, I get to be one of them. I think almost anyone who is bored with print-outs will feel the same.

Watch the North Wind Rise.
Robert Graves. 1949.

7

The Fables of George Ade

A New York man went to visit a Cousin in the Far West. The name of the Town was Fostoria, Ohio.

When he came into Town he had his Watch-Chain on the outside of his Coat, and his Pink Spats were the first ever seen in Fostoria.

"Have you a Manicure Parlor in this Beastly hole?" asked the New York Man, as they walked up from the Train.

"What's that?" asked the Cousin, stepping on his own Feet.

"Great Heavens!" exclaimed the New York Man, and was silent for several Moments.

At Dinner he called for Artichokes, and when told there were none, he said, "Oh, very well," in a Tone of Chastened Resignation.

What you have just read is the beginning of "The Fable of the New York Person Who Gave the Stage Fright to Fostoria, Ohio," one of about five hundred fables written by George Ade between 1897 and 1940. There was no way I could talk about George Ade without beginning by quoting him. He is irresistibly quotable. And not just to casual reviewers, but to Serious Novelists. For example, when Theodore Dreiser was writing *Sister Carrie*, he wanted to describe the traveling salesman that Carrie meets on the way to Chicago in terms that would make instantly clear how deft the fellow was at picking up girls. It was the work of a moment to lift about a page from Ade's "Fable of the Two Mandolin Players and the Willing Performer" and insert it in his text as if written by him. (He did remove most of the capital letters. *Sister Carrie* is written in normal orthography, and the passage would have been Extremely Conspicuous if he had not.)

I don't blame Dreiser for a second, and I understand why he was so hurt when he was accused of plagiarism. What he said in substance was that no one ever *had* described a fast operator so well, and no one ever *would* describe one so well, so it made every kind of sense to use these marvelous words, and he was simply paying George Ade the sincerest of compliments. Besides, they were both from Indiana.

Want to hear the marvelous words? Of course you do. The situation (in Ade, not in Dreiser) is that two conventional young men in Chicago are courting a pretty debutante named Myrtle. They've been courting her for about a year, and as far as they've gotten is that they both call on her every Thursday evening, and play their mandolins (not many stereos in 1899) and make polite conversation. They are too respectful to make any advances. Then a cousin comes on a visit from St. Paul. His name is Gus. He is not respectful at all. Here is how Ade describes him:

He was the Kind of Fellow who would see a Girl twice, and then, upon meeting her the Third Time, he would go up and straighten her Cravat for her, and call her by her First Name.

Put him in a Strange Company—en route to a Picnic—and by the time the Baskets were unpacked he would have a Blonde all to himself, and she would have traded her Fan for his College Pin.

If a Fair-Looker on the Street happened to glance at him Hard he would run up and seize her by the Hand, and convince her that they had Met. And he always Got Away with it, too.

In a Department Store, while waiting for the Cash Boy to come back with the Change, he would find out the girl's Name, her Favorite Flower, and where a Letter would reach her.

Upon entering a Parlor Car at St. Paul he would select a Chair next to the Most Promising One in Sight, and ask her if she cared to have the Shade lowered.

Before the Train cleared the Yards he would have the Porter bringing a Foot-Stool for the Lady.

At Hastings he would be asking her if she wanted Something to Read.

At Red Wing he would be telling her that she resembled Maxine Elliott, and showing her his Watch, left to him by his Grandfather, a Prominent Virginian.

At La Crosse he would be reading the Menu Card to her, and telling her how different it is when you have Some One to join you in a Bite.

At Milwaukee he would go out and buy a Bouquet for her, and when they rode into Chicago they would be looking out of the same Window, and he would be arranging for her Baggage with the Transfer Man. After that they would be Old Friends.

The details are 1899, but the situation is timeless, and if you can read that passage without one or two small shudders of pleasure, then I'm afraid yours is a mind not Open to Humor, and you had better go back to reading the collected works of Richard Nixon and Henry Kissinger.

George Ade was a famous man from a few days after *Fables in Slang* was published until around 1920. Rich, too. He made so much money that he bought up most of his native county in Indiana to have for a hobby—and that was just one of his ways of spending it.

Then he gradually dropped into obscurity—though as late as 1927, some of the fables were being syndicated as a comic strip. There are two reasons, I think. One is that success spoiled him. He published ten volumes of fables in all, and the second five aren't even nearly as good as the first five. People growing up in the twenties, if given a new George Ade book for Christmas by a relative, would wonder what Uncle Henry thought was so funny about *that*, and hurry back to Thurber and Benchley (Benchley I, that is) and other rising stars.

The other is that his vein is a very narrow one. The best hundred or so of his fables are nearly flawless—and they would be even without the capitals, just as e. e. cummings would still be a good poet with them. But in any other form of writing he was just a competent if remarkably prolific writer. (He is thought to have published about twenty-five hundred periodical pieces in his life.) His many sketches of Chicago life read now like sentimental copies of Oliver Wendell Holmes's much earlier sketches of Boston life in *The Autocrat of the Breakfast-Table*. Ade's plays, like *The Sultan of Sulu* and *The College Widow*, made him a lot of money, but they are hopelessly dated. His small body of golden work has gotten lost under this heap of dross.

For a modern reader, free to dig out the best nuggets, there still remains a problem. Ade had the common prejudices of his time and place, and he expressed them (as he did everything) with great freedom. Contemporary readers may be put off by his occasional use of such really quite offensive terms as "coon." A word of advice: keep reading. Sooner or later you will get to the fable of the southern colonel who visits Chicago (this is about 1901) and gets into an altercation with the black headwaiter at his hotel. After the headwaiter has bounced a silver fruit dish off the colonel's head, as reprisal for one of those offensive terms, the colonel pulls out a gun— at which point two other waiters pin his arms, and the cops are called. The Chicago policeman who arrives happens also to be black. "So it came about that He who in Apahatchie County had them trained to hop off the Sidewalk and stand Uncovered until he had passed, now suffered the Hideous Degradation of being marched downstairs by One of Them and then slammed into the Hurry-Up Wagon." He winds up being fined $32.75 (I figure that's about $400 now) and losing his gun.

It is irresistible to quote George Ade. If there were more room, I would probably quote the entire fable of the Stuffer family, prosperous farm folk who move to town and attempt to continue eating in the heroic style to which they had been accustomed—and since it is one of Ade's longest fables as well as one of his funniest, I would wind up seriously unbalancing this book. Instead I'll merely urge you to find out what happened to the New York Person who had them trembling in Fostoria, Ohio. It's not what a complacent easterner might suppose. There is a Turnabout of the most satisfying sort. Ade was good at that.

Fables in Slang.
George Ade. 1899.

8

Falling in Love with Stendhal

Foolish romantic teenagers are always thinking about love. They read about it, too. Look at an issue of *Seventeen*—say, last month's—and you find a regular *leitmotiv*. There's an article called "Eight Love Traps," which tells the foolish teenager how to get out of difficult situations with persons they care for. Another, called "Inching Up to a Shy Person," explains how to get into a new one. There's a quiz article that asks forthrightly "Are You in Love?"

Interest in these matters by no means ceases at age twenty. Glance now at the same month's issue of *Cosmopolitan*. Notice which articles are featured on the cover. One tells "How to Write the Perfect Love Letter." Another, promising considerably more drama, is called "When an Old Friend (Unexpectedly) Becomes a Lover." And for those who didn't learn back when they were teenagers, there is a piece that asks "What Is 'In Love'?"

Interest doesn't even expire at sixty-five. Look at *Modern Maturity*, the magazine of the American Association of Retired Persons, for that same month. There's a lot here about hobbies and health. There's also an article called "Never Too Late to Date."

Most of this stuff is tripe. Tripe with a long heritage, to be sure. That piece on the perfect love letter harks back two and a half centuries to Samuel Richardson, who invented the English novel more or less by accident while he was slapping together a manual on how to write good love (and good other) letters. It may even date back four centuries to when Sir Philip Sidney was biting his pen and looking for the right words to impress young Penelope Devereaux, with whom he was corresponding. The letter wouldn't flow. At that moment he got divine help. The goddess Euterpe dictated to him what must be the shortest (and best) love-letter manual in existence.

"'Fool,' said my Muse to me, 'look in thy heart and write.'"

Sidney is not alone in avoiding tripe. There is a fair amount of distinguished writing on the subject of love. There's Erich Fromm's *The Art of Loving*, for example—not that that focuses on romantic or sexual love. There's Ibn Hazm's eleventh-century work *The Ring of the Dove*—in modern editions subtitled "A Treatise on the Art and Practice of Arab Love." Interesting book, even though the author quotes much too freely from his own poetry. I especially like chapters such as "On Falling in Love While Asleep" (that is, with someone you dream about) and "Of Hinting With the Eyes." There's André le Chapelain's thirteenth-century *The Art of Courtly Love*. There's Ortega y Gasset's *Studies on Love*. All good.

My favorite, though, is a book by the great French novelist Stendhal. *On Love* is a book-length meditation, written long before *The Charterhouse of Parma* or *The Red and the Black*. It has plenty to say about traps, shyness, old friends in new amorous moods, how to know when you're in love—though nothing about dating, which hadn't been invented yet.

Stendhal is pre-Freudian but aware of psychology. He begins by recognizing that love is largely self-generated. The beloved is less a person one meets than a person one creates. This process Stendhal calls crystallization, taking his metaphor from the salt mines of Austria. He had seen miners there stick a bare twig into the saturated water and later pull it out covered with glittering salt diamonds. Before you fall in love, you see the other person as a bare branch; as you fall, you coat him or her with jeweled attractions about 80 percent of your own making.

Next Stendhal turns to classifying the types of love. In his scheme, there are four main ones: passion-love (not what you think), sympathy-love, sensual love (what you think), and vanity-love. Of the four, only passion-love involves full crystallization, and only it truly wins Stendhal's respect.

Vanity-love is the lowest kind. Here you are out to please your own ego, whether through the delight of conquest or through loving someone who will impress your friends and make you envied. The person impresses you too, of course. In Stendhal's own favorite quotation (from the duchesse de Chaulnes in her later years), "A duchess is never more than thirty years old to a snob."

Sensual love comes next. It at least is honest and direct, being sheer physical attraction. But despite our own age's attraction to physical attraction, reverence for the orgasm, etc., Stendhal sees sensual love as fairly minor. Indeed, he claims that much of the time it's just another business transaction, "the only difference being that instead of money we earn pleasure."

Sympathy-love is rather better. This is love by the rules. You know what's expected of you; you have read the manuals, can write perfect love letters, are passionate, casual, tender, playful, brutal, as the rules of your time and your social group demand. Love is here a sport—the best, the most complicated, and the most serious of all sports.

Finally, towering above all these, there is passion-love. You can recognize it by several marks. First, it is never prudent. Not even one little corner of your mind is concerned with whether the person you love will wow your friends, or with how much pleasure you expect to "earn." (Often enough, none.) Second, it transcends self-consciousness. The person who imagines he or she feels passion-love yet tries to preserve dignity is, says Stendhal, "like a man who flings himself from a window and at the same time tries to reach the sidewalk in a graceful attitude." One more: in passion-love, sex is not the goal but a mere antechamber to something better still. As Stendhal says in one of his nicest phrases, in true passion "intimacy [he means in bed] is not so much perfect happiness as the last step toward it."

But the interest of *On Love* does not derive from this tidy classification scheme. It derives from Stendhal's countless asides, anecdotes, and minor insights. For example, have you ever known a married couple where one constantly picks on the other, and yet they stay together for forty years? Stendhal knows exactly why—and analyzes it in the chapter called "Quarrelsome Love." Basically, he says don't feel too sorry for the one who is picked on; he or she gets to star in a life-long drama. "Where could one find, apart from passion-love, gambling, or the possession of power, any other source of daily interest to be compared with it [quarreling] in keenness? If the one who is always finding fault dies, the surviving victim is never consoled. This principle forms the bond of many a middle-class marriage; the person who is nagged at all day long listens to what interests him most."

Or, again, Stendhal has a lot to say about what he calls "failures" and we call male impotence. In fact, the chapter he devotes to failures might well be called "The Stendhal Report on Male Sexuality," and it is fascinating. His thesis is that impotence is not some kind of mechanical failure but (for men) one more test of true love: "If a seed of passion enters into one's soul, there also enters a seed of a possible failure."

He has many stories to tell in support of this theory, such as that of the twenty-three-year-old lieutenant of hussars who, "because he was too much in love, could do nothing but hug his mistress and weep for joy during the first three nights he spent with her." Or take the frank conversation he once had with five handsome young Frenchmen. Except for one, who was almost certainly lying, "we all had *failures* the first time with our most remarkable mistresses." He even tells a story, which I shall not repeat here (I want to tempt you to the book), about the unfortunate and super-romantic colonel in the British Army whom he calls "the king of failures."

That section of the book is every bit as relevant now as it was in 1822. I won't pretend that all sections are. After all, attitudes toward love and sex have undergone at least three major changes since Stendhal wrote: one in early Victorian times, one in the ten years after World War I, and one in the 1960s. Much that Stendhal says is outdated. Furthermore, he wrote as a European to other Europeans, totally ignoring the United States, except to brush us off as a boring new little country that knew nothing of passion-love, being much too occupied with clearing land, making money, and going to church. Beyond that, he wrote as a man to other men; women are not addressed directly in this book.

All the same, if I were a foolish romantic teenager and reasonably literate, or just a person of any age interested in subtle reflections on love, I would step back from the maga-

zine rack and hotfoot it to the nearest library. Or if I had a few
dollars to spare, I'd pop into a bookstore and buy the book,
not even troubling to check which edition they stocked. *On
Love* has been translated well and less well. It doesn't matter.
Like Tolstoy, Stendhal can survive any decent translation.

On Love.
Stendhal. 1822.

9

Moving in Eccentric Circles

In May of 1883 a pretty American girl named Maud Du Puy
arrived in Cambridge, England, to visit relatives. They were
very well-placed relatives indeed. Her Uncle Dick and Aunt
Cara, later Sir Richard and Lady Jebb, knew everyone in the
city worth knowing.

It was a marvelous time for pretty girls to be visiting Cambridge. The faculty at eighteen of the twenty colleges then
making up Cambridge University was 100 percent male—
and, better yet, about 90 percent unmarried. This was not because all those clever men loved celibacy. It was because of
the university rules. For six hundred years after the founding
of Cambridge, the rules said that the fellows of the colleges
must be bachelors, living in college and devoting their time to
study. The only ones allowed to get married were the eighteen
masters of the eighteen men's colleges, the two mistresses of
the two women's colleges, and a few holders of professor-
ships. It wasn't until 1878 that the Revised Statutes came into
effect, and the colleges gradually began to permit ordinary
faculty members to have wives. In 1883, when Maud arrived,
mating fever was at a peak.

Uncle Dick had been a fellow of Trinity College, the largest
and most famous at Cambridge. Naturally his niece met a lot
of the dons at Trinity. By midsummer, no less than three of
them were in hot pursuit.

Maud took this calmly. "The English girls are so *awfully* susceptible," she wrote home; "if a man speaks to them almost, they instantly think he is desperately in love with them." And then she adds, "I am not at all susceptible, and that is one difference between them and me."

Still, one of the three did finally catch her. In 1884, Maud Du Puy was married to George Darwin, second son of the great Charles Darwin, fellow of Trinity, and the newly elected Plumian Professor of Astronomy. (She made him come to Erie, Pennsylvania, for the ceremony.) He was thirty-eight, she twenty-two.

The happy couple—they really were—bought a big house in Cambridge called Newnham Grange and settled down to a high-Victorian life. It was tempered on one side by American independence and on the other by Darwin eccentricity. In due course they had four children. One grew up to marry Lord Keynes, another, named for his grandfather, to be the physicist Sir Charles Darwin (1887–1962), a third to be a distinguished artist.

All this is prologue to *Period Piece*. *Period Piece* is a recollection of that era by one of the participants. Gwen Raverat was the daughter who grew up to be an artist. In this book she tells what it was like to be in that first generation of faculty children, and also what it was like to be a Darwin surrounded by other Darwins. There are few memoirs more charming.

To be a faculty child at Cambridge in the 1880s was to be extraordinarily privileged, and also to be extraordinarily repressed. There was nothing of genteel poverty at Newnham Grange; there was opulence. The house was full of cooks, governesses, and ladies' maids. Its grounds ran along both sides of the river Cam for quite a stretch, and even included two islands in the river, on one of which Maud kept a flock of hens, who had their own private bridge to the shore.

On the other hand, nearly everything a child might want to do was forbidden on principle. It was too dangerous, or it was unrefined, or it was bad for the character. Even bacon for breakfast was bad for the character, and little Gwen Darwin never tasted that delicacy until she was almost ten. "It is true," she adds, "that twice a week we had, at the end of breakfast, one piece of toast, spread with a thin layer of that dangerous luxury, Jam. But, of course, not butter, too. Butter and Jam on the same bit of bread would have been an unheard-of indulgence—a disgraceful orgy."

As for that birthright of even the poorest child in 1988, the candy bar, it was forbidden on two separate grounds. Not only was it held to give the child too much pleasure, it was thought to be unwholesome—loaded by the manufacturer with cheap adulterants. Hence an added thrill of going on trips. The one exception was the butterscotch you could get from penny-in-the-slot machines on railway platforms. "There was a blessed theory that slot machines were pure, that the Railways guaranteed their Virtue."

With local variations from family to family, this sort of thing was common to the whole educated upper middle class in England then, as was the expectation that a girl of six couldn't go outdoors without a hat on, or that one of her natural duties was to be a chaperon to her unmarried aunts and cousins when a gentleman called.

But there was also a special way of life that applied just to Darwins, and it is in describing this that the book reaches its very best. The family that Maud Du Puy married into was large. George Darwin had six brothers and sisters, half of them living in Cambridge. It was also distinguished. Three of the five boys were eventually knighted; nearly everyone was an intellectual. But most of all, it was a family of totally unselfconscious eccentrics. They didn't worry about their images—they almost didn't know they *had* images.

Aunt Etty, Charles Darwin's eldest daughter, was perhaps the supreme eccentric, wearing her extraordinary homemade germ mask ("it tied on like a snout") while receiving visitors. But Uncle William comes close. One of my favorite moments in the book describes his behavior at his father's funeral, which was a state occasion in Westminster Abbey. The question of dignity simply didn't occur to him. "He was sitting in the front seat as eldest son and chief mourner, and he felt a draft on his already bald head; so he put his black gloves to balance on the top of his skull, and sat like that all through the service, with the eyes of the nation upon him."

It is the calm delight that Mrs. Raverat takes in incidents like this that makes her such a joy to read. Her style is remarkable. On the one hand, she had something close to total recall of her childhood— the emotions as well as the events. Many children, myself among them, have thought that no adult understands what it feels like to be a child and have vowed that when *they* grow up, they'll never, ever forget. Few of us manage to keep that vow. She did.

On the other hand, she wrote *Period Piece* when she was in her late sixties, a wise old lady. By then she had come to have that amused but loving tolerance for human failings that I associate with the best kind of grandmothers. The combination of childish immediacy and adult understanding is wonderful. Seldom have so much humor and so little malice coexisted.

The book has one final pleasure. Besides writing the text, Mrs. Raverat drew and captioned about seventy-five illustrations, which come to have a life of their own. They exhibit the same positive delight in the absurdities of human life that the writing does, and the same child's-eye freshness.

If you were going to read only one book in your life about a group of Victorians, I'd say forget Lytton Strachey, even forget Steven Marcus's *The Other Victorians*. Forget Lady Longford and Margaret Drabble. Read *Period Piece*.

Period Piece.
Gwen Raverat. 1953.

10

Lament for a Young Wife

There are a handful of poets who are known only for a single line. Take John Burgon, whose collected poems appeared in London in 1885. The name fails to ring a bell? You bet it does. Poor Burgon had just one moment of glory (as a poet) in his entire life. Back when he was a student, 40 years earlier, he had won the Newdigate Prize at Oxford for a long poem called "Petra." It has enjoyed a deserved neglect ever since. All but the 132d line, which reads:

A rose-red city, half as old as time.

That line is still current. It's in hundreds of books of quotations. (There are hundreds, too. If you think there's just Bartlett, you haven't been looking.) It's also quoted fairly often in commercial writing. The rose-red city is a real place, a glorious ruin in the kingdom of Jordan, and tourist ads use the line as part of their come-on.

It even figures in literature. The great Irish fantasy writer Lord Dunsany once built a whole story around Burgon's line. The narrative takes place in heaven. There are (Dunsany says) numerous cliques in heaven, including a quite exclusive literary club, which admits only major poets. One day Shakespeare, Goethe, and the others are surprised to see a completely unfamiliar face. Guess whose. He got in for his one line.

A somewhat larger number of poets survive through a single work. For example, the Jesuit poet Jean Baptiste Gresset (1709–77) is remembered almost exclusively for the poem "Vert Vert," the story of a parrot who lives in a French convent. Peter Motteux (1663–1718), once famous in London as poet, dramatist, and translator of *Don Quixote*, is now known only for the roundelay that begins

> Man is for the woman made, and the woman for the man

But the greatest of the one-poem survivors is, I think, Henry King, an Englishman born in 1592. His "Exequy to His Matchless Never-to-be-Forgotten Friend" is quite simply one of the supreme laments in our language.

The friend that King promised never to forget was his wife Anne. She died young. She was twenty-four (and he thirty-two); they had been joyfully married since she was sixteen. Soon after her death he wrote his great poem.

King was a metaphysical poet, like his close friend and fellow clergyman John Donne, and he uses the extravagant language of the metaphysicals throughout "The Exequy." But this one poem would suffice, if it had to, to show that extravagant language and enormous metaphors can coexist with total sincerity and with the deepest of deep feelings.

After a beginning in which King represents himself standing in front of his wife's grave, he begins to address her directly.

> Dear Loss! since thy untimely fate
> My task hath been to meditate
> On Thee, on Thee!

Already one sees what a strength the second person singular once was to our language. Poignancy is possible with "you," but it's harder.

He then tells his wife that since she died time has slowed to a crawl. Not because he didn't have anything to do. He had three small children to raise alone, an important job as Archdeacon of Colchester, frequent sermons to preach at Saint Paul's Cathedral in London. None of this cheers him.

> I languish out, not Live the Day,
> Using no other Exercise
> But what I practice with mine Eyes.
> By which wet glasses I find out
> How lazily Time creeps about
> To one that mourns.

This is the first of his extravagant metaphors—comparing his tear-filled eyes to wet hourglasses, which take forever to measure out a single hour of time. It is nothing to what follows. Next he compares his wife to the sun, now gone down, and himself to a man alone on the darkened earth.

> Thou hast benighted me. Thy set
> This Eve of blackness did beget,
> Who wast my Day, (though overcast
> Before thou hadst thy Noon-tide past)
> And I remember must in tears,
> Thou scarce hadst seen so many years
> As day tells hours.

There would seem to be a problem with this metaphor, since in reality the sun never sets in the morning, and he has just said that his wife died before reaching the noon of her life. There isn't, though. King deftly takes the metaphor and twists it. His sun didn't set, he now says, it was most unnaturally eclipsed. By what? By the earth—and he is simultaneously talking about astronomy and about the fact that his wife's body is buried in the earth.

Then he begins to wish that the eclipse would pass, and the sun come out again.

> I could allow thee for a time
> To darken me and my sad Clime,
> Were it a month, a year, or ten,
> I would thy Exile live till then;
> And all that space my mirth adjourn.
> So thou wouldst promise to return.

But of course he knows that she can't promise, that this eclipse
will not end, that he will not see her again as long as he lives.
He gives the metaphor another twist, and begins to envy the
very soil she is buried in. It is nearer to her now than he is.

> Meantime, thou hast her, Earth: much good
> May my harm do thee. Since it stood
> With Heaven's will I might not call
> Her longer mine, I give thee all
> My short-liv'd right and interest
> In her, whom living I loved best:
> With a most free and bounteous grief,
> I give thee what I could not keep.

A powerful line, that last one.

Now he changes metaphors. In fact, the change took place
during the passage I've just quoted. From being the eclipser
of his sun, the earth turns into a rival, an almost human rival.
And playing daringly with the idea of bodily resurrection (at
the Last Judgement he *will* see her again), he tells the earth
that she is not a gift after all, but only a loan. On the last day
he will come to reclaim her. When he does, he will hold the
earth sternly to account that none of her be lost. He might be
a Renaissance banker talking to a client.

> See that thou make thy reck'ning straight,
> And yield her back again by weight;
> For thou must audit on thy trust
> Each grain and atom of this Dust;
> As thou wilt answer *Him*, that leant,
> Not gave thee, my dear Monument.

Having dismissed his rival, King now turns and speaks again to his wife. Full of the idea that she will rise from her grave warm and breathing, the same young wife that he lost, he begs her to wait for him in the churchyard, by her empty tomb.

> Stay for me there: I will not fail
> To meet thee in that hollow Vale.
> And think not much of my delay
> I am already on the way.

The tone has changed, and the rest of the poem is a series of variations on the now-triumphant thought that he is sure to join her. And now he uses yet another metaphor: he compares himself to a ship sailing westward—to death and to her.

> Each minute is a short Degree
> And ev'ry hour a step towards thee.
> At night when I betake to rest,
> Next morn I rise nearer my West
> Of Life, almost by eight hours' sail
> Than when Sleep breathed his drowsy gale.

Time has speeded up again.

And so he can end the poem almost happily.

> I am content to live
> Divided, with but half a Heart,
> Till we shall Meet and never Part.

People who enjoy cheap irony might enjoy hearing that a year or two after writing this Henry King got married again. He was very eligible: young, handsome, and wealthy. Furthermore, remembering those three small children, he had the most practical of reasons to find a new wife. But it didn't happen. He lived on for forty-five years, a busy and promi nent man. He served as the executor of John Donne's estate; he became Dean of Rochester, then Bishop of Chichester. He

died "the epitome of all honours, virtues, and generous no-
bleness." But he never remarried.

A part of me—the twentieth century part—is a little sad
about that. Forty-five years is a long time to live alone. He
could have had two or three more nice marriages. But another
part of me rejoices that art and life should have come together
here; that what Henry King wrote in a great poem should also
have been the deepest impulse of his being; that he kept his
promise.

"The Exequy."
Henry King. 1624.

11

Thinking Rabbits and Talking Crows

Until just the other day, Canadian literature hardly existed. I mean, a literature that had Louis Honoré Fréchette and Bliss Carman for its two leading poets, and that couldn't do much better than T. C. Haliburton and Louis Hémon as novelists, was distinctly minor league. It was ahead of, say, Guatemalan literature, but not much.

There were exceptions, of course. There are always exceptions. One was the great naturalist who wrote first as Ernest Seton Thompson and later as Ernest Thompson Seton. (The change was roughly comparable to Irving Wallace's son becoming David Wallechinsky. Seton's Scottish great-grandfather, fleeing with a price on his head after the battle of Culloden, had disguised himself with the first English-sounding name he thought of, which happened to be Thompson. Seton wanted to reclaim his identity.)

He also wanted to and did lead a remarkably diverse life. He grew up partly on the Manitoba frontier, partly in stuffy Toronto. As a young man he was a professional wolf hunter, both in Canada and New Mexico. But he also studied art in Paris—and more than studied: he had a picture accepted for the Salon in 1891. He published scores of scientific articles on the wildlife of Manitoba. He went to New York and drew all the natural history illustrations for *The Century Dictionary*. He helped to found the Boy Scouts, and served as Chief

Scout until he resigned in disgust when Theodore Roosevelt got the idea of giving the lads military training.

The thing he did best, though, was to write stories. He could do human characters—his novel of frontier boyhood, *Two Little Savages*, is still a delight—but nearly all his best work is about animals. The best, or some of it, is to be found in *Wild Animals I have Known*.

The book tells the stories of eight very different animals. There's Lobo, the greatest of the wolves he went to hunt in New Mexico; Silverspot, a crow living in pine woods just north of Toronto; Wully, a sheepdog who led a secret life at night as a sheep killer; Raggylug, a young rabbit living on the edge of a Manitoba farm, and so on. Kipling once said it was reading the story of Raggylug that gave him the idea for *The Jungle Book*.

Seton loved heroes, and in one way or another each of these animals is heroic. Not anthropormorphized, much less Disneyfied, just heroic. Lobo, for example, the giant leader of the Currumpaw wolves, can and does outsmart men with traps, poison baits, and packs of dogs. Silverspot led a flock of two hundred crows for more than twenty years—taught the young ones each year how to deal with owls, hawks and men with guns, and even how to distinguish between a man with an umbrella and a man with a gun. Raggylug leads nobody— cottontail rabbits are not herd animals—but he has mastered the art of luring a dog into a barbed wire fence, and his fight with an older rabbit who moves into the swamp where he lives is a real epic.

Heroic animals are hardly scarce in literature. Where they are scarce is in books by naturalists—who indeed are much more apt to discuss populations of animals rather than individuals, heroic or otherwise. What gives Seton his appeal is the combination of exciting and sometimes even melodramatic stories with meticulous and authoritative detail. The detail had every right to be meticulous. After all, Seton had written a manual called *Birds of Manitoba* in 1891; he had published another book called *Art Anatomy of Animals* in 1896; it was a painting of a sleeping wolf that got admitted to the Salon. He knew what he was talking about, and in the hundreds of little marginal sketches that are one of the great charms of his books, he knew what he was drawing. If he says that crows have blue eyes when young and brown eyes when full grown, or that male rabbits rub their chins as high up as they can reach on small trees, and thus leave a scent mark for other male rabbits to investigate, or that dogs cannot be induced to hunt she-wolves during mating season, you know that you are getting facts.

Seton himself claimed a good deal more than that. "These stories are true" are the very first words of *Wild Animals I Have Known*. He meant them to apply not just to the background detail but to the remarkable stories he tells: Lobo running across the backs of a huddled flock of sheep to get at the handful of goats in the middle, knowing that once he has killed the goats the sheep will stampede. A mother fox who comes every night right into a barnyard to nurse her captive cub and try to free him but who, once she realizes she cannot gnaw through the metal chain or dig it loose, kills her son rather than leave him in captivity. A crow leader who has ten different calls, each with a specific and translatable meaning. "Ca-ca-ca-ca caw," for example (which Seton gives complete with musical notation) means "Great danger—a gun," while "C-r-r-r-a-w" means roughly "Let's mate." That same crow able to count up to thirty, and the average crow in his flock able to count up to six.

When I was a boy reading Seton's books, it never occurred to me to doubt any of this—not even when Lobo, the wolf no man was smart enough to kill, winds up dying for love of his mate, the white wolf Blanca. I simply rejoiced that such things existed in the world and wished *I* had the eyes to see them.

It occurred to other natural scientists in Seton's time, though, and eventually one of the greatest of them went on the attack. In 1903, John Burroughs denounced Seton in print. What he said in effect was that Seton tells wonderful stories, but why does he insist on claiming they're true? Then he began listing the lies in *Wild Animals I Have Known*. Being himself an expert ornithologist, he went especially hard at the story of Silverspot. He said, for example, that crows don't *have* leaders; that they can't count to six, let alone thirty; that while they undoubtedly have "various calls," no human being could possibly know what they mean, still less render them in English.

I suspect that Burroughs was partly right. Some of the stories Seton tells are simply too good to be true. But I know for certain that he wasn't entirely right. Later scientists have vindicated at least one of Seton's observations. Seton says that Silverspot could convey ten different messages, does he? David Johnson, in *The Biosystematics of American Crows* (1961), notes calmly that crows are capable of "no less than 10 different kinds of notes or calls." He offers no translations. But Franklin Coombs does, in a 1978 book called *The Crows*. Not in Seton's dramatic terms, and only of five crow-cries, but still translations.

The wonderful thing about Seton is that he offers a middle road between the frank sentimentalism of *Bambi* and ten thousand other children's books, and the impersonal statistics of most bioresearch. I'm pretty sure that, as Huckleberry

Finn would say, he tells a few stretchers, but the animal hero-ism and cleverness and, yes, emotion that he describes are real things. The stories he embodies them in are superb. Even Burroughs granted that. What child could ask for more?

Well, there is one more thing a child could ask for. He (or she—my daughters love Seton) could ask that a book this good stay in print, so that he or she could get it as a Christmas present. Canadian publishers, to their credit, *have* kept *Wild Animals I Have Known* steadily in print. In the United States it is sometimes available, sometimes not. Right now it is, which is cause for rejoicing. But even now one's joy is quali-fied. The book has a masterly successor called *Biography of a Grizzly* and a fine sequel called *Lives of the Hunted*, both of which any child would naturally wish to read right afterwards. Both are about to appear as paperbacks and if we are lucky will stay in print several years. But after that? If the past is any guide, they will revert to being available only in one of those library-edition reprints that seem to have been priced by the people who price Godiva chocolates or Gucci purses. I mean, a quite ordinary edition cost around $40. Pity.

Wild Animals I Have Known.
Ernest Thompson Seton. 1898.

12

Taking Ghosts Seriously

There is a lot of writing (and filming) about the super-natural going on currently, nearly all of it cynical. It's cynical in the sense that the authors don't believe for a second that there really might be a vampire lurking in Rock Creek Park in Washington, D. C., or that some large dog is possessed by the powers of evil. All they believe in is the marketability of plots like that. Such cynicism has a price. Almost inevitably their books and movies come out shallow.

Serious writing about the supernatural is quite another matter. That can wind up deeper and more powerful than al-most anything else in our literature. *The Divine Comedy*, for example, or *Beowulf*. The reason is obvious. A universe in which the supernatural operates is a universe charged with meaning. And to invest action with meaning is perhaps the most important thing literature does.

Charles Williams's novel *All Hallows Eve* is one of the most powerful works of supernaturalism to appear in our century. It comes, appropriately enough, out of the same nexus as many other such works: *The Lord of the Rings*, *Perelandra*, the Narnian chronicles. Williams was a friend and contempo-rary of Tolkien and C. S. Lewis—and when his work took him to Oxford during the Second World War, he promptly became the third great central figure in the informal literary group known as the Inklings.

Williams is not nearly so well known as Lewis and Tolkien, and there are several reasons. One is that most of the time he is not nearly so good a writer. Another is that he's a much better mystic than either of them—and mystics make harder and higher demands on their readers than story tellers (Tolkien) and allegorists (Lewis). A third is that unlike them Williams does not write the kind of fiction available to both children and adults, but a kind available to adults only. *All Hallows Eve* will never be a TV special—or if it is, it will be so debased and vulgarized as to make most TV specials of great books seem works of astonishing fidelity.

The book opens in London in 1945. The war has just ended. A loving young wife named Lester Furnival is waiting on Westminster Bridge to meet Richard, her husband of six months. There is a strange lull over the city as she waits, not a sound to be heard, not another person in sight. Finally, just as she is impatiently leaving the bridge to search for him, Richard comes walking into sight. His face goes white when he sees her, and then he springs toward her.

But she is angry at having had to wait so long; she throws up a hand to repel him. The gesture has extraordinary force. Richard is driven backward by it as if by a wind. As he vanishes, Lester realizes that for the moment they were together, the sounds of the city had returned. Now they fade again. It is then that she realizes she is dead. It takes her somewhat longer to realize that she is in what Williams always calls The City, one of many mystical cities that coexist with the actual living London of 1945 (and of 1988). Most of the newly dead are in that City, though rarely present to each other, since for each of them it is a slightly different place, depending on what each valued in life.

But people who die together are likely to enter The City together, and Lester had been with her friend Evelyn when an airplane crashed on the bridge and killed them. The two young women soon encounter. It is not an easy or a happy meeting. The disguises that masked their friendship when they were alive are gone. It is clear to both of them that Lester, who was a much more vivid and interesting person, had been a kind of fire at which Evelyn warmed herself. And clear that for Lester Evelyn had been a convenience, someone to call if she happened to want company when she went shopping. Clear, in short, that each had used the other. One main theme in the book is the progressive salvation of Lester and the progressive damnation of Evelyn as they face what they were, and do or don't decide to change.

But it is by no means the only theme. *All Hallows Eve* has a complex and even thrilling plot. The action swirls around a great religious leader named Simon Leclerc: a prophet, a worker of miracles, the head of a world cult. He is something like the Reverend Mr. Moon raised to the fourth power—or he seems that way to outsiders at least. He is actually the most powerful magician who has lived in several hundred years, and he is a tall, god-like, ascetic, and wholly evil person, a negative of Jesus Christ, whose very distant cousin he in fact is. What he promises human beings is peace; what he actually seeks is to rule them, not only in life but even after their deaths.

All the other characters meet Simon, and all in the end must choose between serving him and resisting him. Richard, Lester's husband, meets him because Richard is a British diplomat, and Simon has become so great a force that the government must deal with him almost as if he were another country. Lester and Evelyn meet him through his daughter, who spends many of her nights in the mystical city.

This tormented girl of twenty-one needs some explaining. She has no idea that she is Simon's daughter. Her name is Betty Wallingford, and she supposes her father to be Air Marshal Sir Bartholomew Wallingford, a man who has exercised his fatherhood chiefly in being away on duty with the RAF. Her mother, Lady Wallingford, is the prophet's chief disciple, and a formidable woman.

Betty is not the result of clandestine passion. Simon and Lady Wallingford slept together once only, and that for the specific purpose of producing a child of his flesh over whose spirit he will have a special control.

With the willing consent of Lady Wallingford, Simon has for some years been putting Betty into night trances, forcing her soul out of her body, and sending it into The City, where past, present and future are, if not one, at least intermixed. Through her eyes he can see several months ahead. This increases the accuracy of his prophecies greatly . . . and the only cost is the steady deterioration of his daughter's health. No problem there; he intends to kill her soon anyway—just as soon as his control is complete. Then her soul is to be stationed permanently in The City to serve as his agent.

A sheer accident frustrates this plan. Years ago, Betty happened to attend the same girls' boarding school as Lester and Evelyn—and in fact to have been Evelyn's chosen victim among the younger girls. That fact, too, has force in The City, and the two dead women perceive the living visitor, and follow her home. One of them soon joins Simon; the other sets herself to save Betty. Few supernatural struggles, I think, have been more splendidly portrayed. The climax comes in a great ritual, half magic and half Christian, on All Hallows Eve, more commonly known in this country as Hallowe'en.

Badly summarized this way, the book sounds downright lurid. It isn't. It is solemn and august and even a little bit holy. Best of all, it succeeds in making The City a place more real than the earth we live on. Words spoken there are almost palpable. When Evelyn, soon after the crash, is protesting the unfairness of everything, she whines to Lester, "Why are we here like this? I haven't done anything. I haven't; I tell you, I haven't. I haven't done *anything*." And Charles Williams adds, "The last word rose like a wail in the night, almost (as in the old tales) as if a protesting ghost was loosed and fled, in a cry as thin as its own tenuous wisp of existence, through the irresponsive air of a dark world, where its own justification was its only, and worst, accusation." That is, Evelyn in protesting that she hadn't done anything was using the phrase in its conventional sense, to mean that she had done nothing wrong. But in The City the literal meaning inheres in the words (and is true)—that in her twenty-five years of life she had been almost entirely passive and inert, that she had wasted the gift of being.

Or again, Lester, trying to rouse her friend into doing something now, exclaims at one point, "Oh, my God!"

"It was," Williams says, "the kind of exclamation she and Richard had been in the habit of throwing about all over the place. It meant nothing; when they were seriously aggressive or aggrieved, they used language borrowed from bestiality or hell. She had never thought it meant anything. But in this air every word meant something, meant itself; and this curious new exactitude of speech hung there like a strange language, as if she had sworn in Spanish or Pushtu, and the oath had echoed into an invocation." Everything in The City is like that, and it makes The City an exciting if scary place to visit.

Philip Larkin speaks in his greatest poem (which you'll encounter later in this book) of people in the twentieth century surprising in themselves a hunger to be more serious than they are. For anyone with that hunger, *All Hallows Eve* is a magical book indeed.

All Hallows Eve.
Charles Williams. 1944.

13

The Decline and Fall of Switzerland

The decline and fall of the Roman Empire has been the subject of much good literature, from Gibbon's six-volume history to Auden's tiny brilliant poem. It's not hard to see why. That long decline and eventual crash is not only one of the supreme dramas of history, it is one charged with special significance for the twentieth century. It is in the West, anyway. We wonder uneasily if our own decline began in 1914, if we are Europeans, or somewhere around 1965, if we are Americans. We may even look around for a Caesar or a president who will assure us it hasn't.

Bryher's novel *Roman Wall* is thus part of a long tradition. But it differs from most other books about the dying empire in one very striking way. Most of them give some kind of overview. They tell the story from the center, as the CIA would have known it, if the Romans had had a CIA. Consuls and tribunes and vast armies play their splendid parts.

Rome is barely mentioned in *Roman Wall*. The great city in this book is a place called Aventicum, which most of us have never heard of. (It survives to this day as a Swiss village of a couple of thousand called Avenches, which most of us have never heard of either.)

It is historic fact that in 265 A.D. German tribes—the Alemanni—crossed the Rhine and captured the Helvetian frontier city of Augusta Raurica. Half a legion perished in one day. Pausing only to loot and burn, the tribes moved on to beseige Aventicum, the provincial capital. That also rapidly fell. Its garrison died in the burning temple. The city was never rebuilt, though the mere ruins remained enough to impress Byron fifteen centuries later.

Around this minor incident in a minor Roman province (Gibbon never mentions it), Bryher has written a wonderful novel. Reading it, it is hard to remember that she was actually a woman of our own time, and not an eyewitness to those far-off events.

The story has two sets of main characters. One set consists of a Roman centurion named Valerius, his sister Julia, and their small household of two free-born Helvetians and several slaves. Valerius has not had a successful career. As a very young officer, fourteen years earlier, he had an affair with the wife of his commanding officer, and got caught. Banished to the frontier, he now commands an outpost of only fifteen men. He and Julia couldn't even afford the modest villa they live in if it weren't for the fact that real estate prices are steadily dropping in that part of Switzerland, as the threat of invasion increases.

The other set consists of the governor of the province, his wife-in-all-but-name, and several members of his far larger household. And linking the two sets, a traveling Greek merchant named Demetrius. Demetrius spends his winters in Verona, but each spring he sets out with a train of mules and slaves to sell amber, furs, perfume, and other luxuries in the provinces. He is a good man: honest, very intelligent, by the standards of the third century kind to his slaves. He also, you gradually learn, gets his best furs from the Alemanni, paying for them with Roman weapons. That practice is totally forbidden, and quite widespread.

Since the entire story takes place in the year that Aventicum fell, it is obviously an exciting one. It would make a good movie—I can think of twenty gloriously filmable scenes without even trying—and perhaps someday a smart producer will take notice.

But plot is the least of the book's strengths. More impressive is the extraordinary texture of reality. There is not one character whose actions and thought processes do not seem to me at once alien (these people lived seventeen hundred years ago) and true. Take Valerius the centurion and his sister Julia. They are conservatives, imbued with the old-Roman ideas of dignity and propriety. Valerius is prepared to die uselessly at his outpost unless he gets orders to evacuate, even though he knows the governor is a heavy drinker and very apt to forget details in a crisis. Julia, a beautiful woman around thirty, will not marry the high-ranking officer who seeks her, because she feels tainted by her brother's disgrace. At the same time, Valerius is a comfort-loving man who must have his nap after lunch and his bought Swiss girls but also a true mystic whose long-ago affair was as much religious experience as it was sexual consummation. Julia is neurotic—an anal-retentive in Freud's terms—scrubbing the mosaic floor in the kitchen of their villa until she actually dislodges tiles; and she is also a woman of deep power, drawn to the austere rites of Apollo.

Or take Felix, the one Christian in the book. Felix is the overseer for Demetrius's trade caravan, a slave for most of his life who has recently managed to buy his freedom. (Demetrius had to pay the government a tax on the purchase price.) Felix is a convert, a true believer. But he is also a very bad Christian by modern standards because he is so full of hatred. He is not about to forgive *anybody*, especially not Romans. When he goes to confession in Verona in the winter, he has to—and does—lie to the priest about his feelings in order to get absolution. These are complex characters.

More impressive still are the ways in which Bryher shows the powerful but decaying society in which these characters move. Shows, not discusses. She never preaches or teaches. Rather, the decadence emerges in glimpses such as Demetrius meeting Alemanni chieftains in secret, or a well-bred youth being ostentatiously bored at the gladiatorial games in Aventicum ("two Thracians slashing at each other")—he is too civilized to take the empire seriously.

And most impressive of all, Bryher manages to convey a subtle sense of *why* the empire is beginning to decay. She does not, like Gibbon, pin it on Christianity; what she suggests is that the sheer size of the empire is mainly responsible. The virtues that made early Rome great are by no means lost; they are just increasingly out of place in vast anonymous world-power Rome, even as the old virtues of participatory democracy seem to be increasingly an impediment in vast anonymous world-power America. (This is my comparison, not hers. The characters in *Roman Wall* sometimes look back from 265 A.D.; they never cheat and look ahead.)

Bryher was really an Englishwoman named Winifred Ellerman. She took her pen name when she first began to write, in part because her father, Sir John Ellerman, Bt., was a power in English publishing, and she scorned to trade on that fact. During a long and adventurous life, she became a poet and an avant-garde film critic as well as a novelist. But her special genius was for portraying ancient societies as they died, or perhaps were painfully reborn. *Gate to the Sea* is a fine example, an almost magical evocation of the conquered Greek city of Poseidonia around 300 B.C. But *Roman Wall* is her masterpiece.

Roman Wall.
Bryher. 1954.

14

Gulliver Goes to Washington

In the fall of 1879, a brilliant young widow named Madeleine Lee moved from New York to Washington, D.C. Her twin objects: to observe the workings of the United States government, and to meet great men. Or at least to see if Washington has any *to* meet.

Mrs. Lee has found greatness to be in very short supply in New York. The New York men she knows all seem to be stockbrokers. Millionaires, many of them, but lacking in ideas. She is rich herself (her $30,000 a year would easily equal $300,000 a year now), and mere wealth does not impress her.

When she visits Boston, it's no better. There are scholars and artists in society there, to be sure, well bred and prosperous, but they mainly strike her as dilettantes. "You are just like the rest of us," she tells a Boston friend. "You grow six inches high, and then you stop. Why will not somebody grow to be a tree, and cast a shadow?" Some months later it occurs to her that a U.S. senator or the president might cast a shadow. Hence her move.

So begins the best political novel yet written in America, Henry Adams's *Democracy*. The author had extraordinary qualifications for writing it. His own family had been casting shadows for three generations. His great-grandfather, while

72

serving as president of the United States, was the one who supervised the transfer of the government to Washington in 1800. His grandfather had been both president and a congressman. His father had been both ambassador to England and a congressman. (Well, actually minister to England—in those days we were a more modest nation.)

Henry Adams himself was a writer, not a politician, but he knew politics inside out. One of his boyhood memories was the exciting nomination of his father for vice-president on the Free Soil ticket. As a young man he had the opportunity to study government on both sides of the Atlantic—first as a congressional aide in Washington for a winter, then for seven years as an American diplomat in London.

At all times he had something close to total entrée. He hadn't been a congressional aide for a week before he was sharing after-dinner cigars and political confidences with Senator William H. Seward of New York, probably the most powerful man in Congress. That was the winter of 1860, and Adams was twenty-two. Leaders in England were almost equally accessible. And when he returned to Washington as a journalist in 1868, the city opened itself to him like an oyster. The attorney general of the United States insisted on putting him up until he could find an apartment. The secretary of state found the apartment for him.

He was not your common journalist.

In returning to Washington in 1868, Adams was doing exactly what he had Madeleine Lee do in the novel. He was studying the workings of democracy, and he was looking for great men. What he found, of course, was the beginning of the Grant administration and a terrible disillusionment. He already knew that nineteenth-century politics were corrupt, in England and America both, but the scandals of Grant's first year were exceptional. That was the year that Jay Gould almost succeeded in using the United States government as a servant to help him corner the gold market.

Adams was outraged at the corruption, disgusted with the folly, and contemptuous of the social climbing he saw in Washington. In letters written that year, he freely expressed his anger. In the *Education of Henry Adams*, written late in life, it appeared in congealed form, as corrosive irony. But in between, when he wrote *Democracy*, a wonderful thing happened. That anger was transmuted into almost perfect comedy. The comedy plays over everything Mrs. Lee sees and much that she doesn't: the selection of a new presidential cabinet, senatorial dinners, eager young reformers, pretty blonde lobbyists with no scruples.

Perhaps the funniest scene is the one that describes Washington snobbery. Toward the end of the book, Lord Skye, the British minister, gives a gala ball in honor of the grand duke and duchess of Saxe-Baden-Hombourg. He has to, because the grand duchess was born an English princess. Because he knows that everybody who is anybody will want to come, and that the British Legation though large is finite, Lord Skye cleverly waits until Congress has recessed. Then he issues invitations with a lavish hand. Among others, he invites

all the senators, all the representatives in Congress, all the governors of States with their staffs, if they had any, all eminent citizens and their families throughout the Union and Canada, and finally every private individual from the North Pole to the Isthmus of Panama, who had ever shown him a civility, or was able to control interest enough to ask for a card. The result was that Baltimore promised to come in a body, and Philadelphia was equally well disposed; New York provided several scores of guests, and Boston sent the governor and a delegation; even the well-known millionaire who represented California in the United States Senate was irritated because his invitation having been timed to arrive just one day too late, he was prevented from bringing his family across the continent with a choice party in a director's car.

Many things happen at that ball, including a proposal to Mrs. Lee and a glorious success on the dance floor for her twenty-four-year-old sister Sybil, the mere description of whose dress is one of the most charming pieces of writing I know. The main action, though, is right out of Lewis Carroll.

Naturally the president and his wife are present. As it happens, the president is a former Indiana farmer (and state governor) known to his friends as Old Granite and to his enemies as Old Granny. His wife is both strong minded and very puritanical. She and the grand duchess—equally strong minded—take an instant dislike to each other; in fact, they declare war. Result: all evening the two women are seated on identical sofas, on opposite sides of the ballroom, the royal insignia above one, and the American eagle above the other—two angry queens on thrones. Each wishes to prevent all the more important guests from talking to the other, and so each gathers them around her sofa, as one might take chess pieces. It is a splendid piece of writing.

But *Democracy* cuts deeper than that. Under the surface, it is also a serious look at American government as Madeleine gradually comes to understand it. And here the book operates on no less than three levels.

When Madeleine arrives in Washington, she very quickly meets an authentic great man. His name is Silas P. Ratcliffe; he is a senator from Illinois, and he is the leading Republican in the country, more powerful even than Old Granny. Both literally and figuratively, he is very much more than six inches tall. In fact, he is known as the Prairie Giant of Peonia. He is fifty years old and a widower.

Partly through her beauty and intelligence, and partly by going to hear him in the Senate and telling him afterwards that he speaks as well as Daniel Webster (he "rose to this gaudy fly like a huge, two-hundred-pound salmon"), Madeleine soon has Senator Ratcliffe in love with her. He is not just in love but eagerly sharing the dilemmas of government. For a time Madeleine is deeply impressed.

Meanwhile, another, less obviously great man has fallen in love with her: an incorruptible Virginia lawyer named Carrington, who is a kind of collateral descendant of George Washington. Carrington recognizes Senator Ratcliffe's greatness but knows that it is the greatness of mere ambition. He also knows what is otherwise a well-kept secret: Ratcliffe once took a $100,000 payment from a steamship company. (A handsome sum indeed. Equal to twenty years' salary. U.S. senators were paid $5,000 a year at the time.) Carrington is determined to prevent Madeleine from marrying the Prairie Giant. So, for quite different reasons, is old Baron Jacobi, the Bulgarian Minister. The central plot of the book concerns this struggle over Madeleine Lee.

On the top level, Adams wrote a *roman á clef*. Senator Ratcliffe was modeled on James G. Blaine, a great (and corrupt) Republican leader. Similarly, Old Granny is a wickedly funny amalgam of Presidents U.S. Grant and Rutherford B. Hayes. Even Baron Jacobi was drawn from that remarkable Turkish diplomat and man-about-nineteenth-century-Washington, Aristarchi Bey. Blaine, incidentally, recognized himself easily when the book came out, and was furious.

That level is minor. More important is the next level, on which Adams evaluates the men—and women—one meets in public life. The book says there are three kinds to meet in Washington: boorish Americans, civilized Americans, and Europeans. The boorish Americans, by no coincidence, considering where Adams came from, are mostly midwesterners. The civilized Americans are mostly easterners. The Europeans are mostly diplomats.

All three classes are absurd, though not equally so. The

worst are boorish Americans. They're so absurd that Madeleine doesn't even bother to know any—so that the only detailed studies you get in the book (besides Ratcliffe) are the president and his wife, whom she can't avoid knowing. Granny and Mrs. G are not just stupid and narrow. They actively dislike good taste or intelligence. Insofar as the book is a comedy, they are treated completely as figures of fun.

Adams does allow Old Granny one good trait. He is honest, as was Grant. But his honesty is perfectly useless, because he is too stupid to be effectual. It takes Senator Ratcliffe exactly one week to get control of him and hence of the new administration. So much for Nature's Nobleman, or the Great American Boor.

Class two comprises the civilized Americans. Many of them are stupid, too, such as Mr. C. C. French, the reforming Congressman from Connecticut, or Mr. Schneidekoupon (it translates Mr. Coupon Clipper), the rich, well-bred, dumb Philadelphia financier.

But there are many smart ones, too. One is Mr. Nathan Gore, the poet and historian from Boston who has just been our minister to Spain and who is in Washington trying to wangle a new appointment. (His real-life model was the historian John Motley.) Mr. Gore is infinitely more amusing to talk to than Old Granny. But he is also, as Madeleine perceives him, "abominably selfish, colossally egoistic, and not a little vain." And he is prepared to kneel down and lick Ratcliffe's boots if that will help him get back into office. In short, he is little more than an American boor with a good education. Adams treats him with scorn.

Class three is made up of the Europeans. They are the most civilized of all, but that doesn't keep them from being absurd. Count Popoff and Count Orsini, despite their Russian and Italian sophistication, are a couple of young nincompoops, and the visiting Irish peer, Lord Dunbeg, though nicer, isn't greatly smarter. He and Old Granny, so different in many ways, are alike in having limited perceptions. He is still well ahead of the grand duchess.

Adams is saying that Madeleine goes to Washington and finds that people are six inches tall there too. The rulers of Saxe-Baden-Hombourg are six inches tall; the president is six inches tall; Senator Krebs of Pennsylvania (the name means "crabs") is perhaps only five inches tall. *Democracy* is a kind of modern *Gulliver's Travels*, and we see Madeleine in the role of Gulliver; she is in the capital of Lilliput, surrounded by spiritual dwarves.

But there are four exceptions: Ratcliffe, Carrington, Baron Jacobi, and the British Minister, Lord Skye—one boorish American, one civilized American, and two Europeans who are full-sized people.

The action of the book is the triumph of the civilized characters over the boor. As social comedy, *Democracy* is very much in the genteel tradition, and it has a good many snobbish elements. Madeleine and Sybil and Lord Skye and Carrington all know when it is correct to wear gloves; Ratcliffe and Old Granny don't. Ratcliffe also doesn't know French or anything about art. What he does know is how to stuff ballot boxes, take bribes, control congressmen, and win elections. He is a giant, but a smelly one. The reader is delighted when Carrington and Jacobi set out in their separate ways to prevent Madeleine from marrying him. She has been ready to, because she has the illusion, which Ratcliffe cleverly abets, that she will be able to civilize him and help him to be, one day, a great and honorable president.

On this level, *Democracy* is a happy book with a happy ending. Carrington *does* thwart Senator Ratcliffe, and there is even a scene, which Adams must have loved writing, where the old roué Jacobi cracks Ratcliffe over the head with his cane. Culture and breeding triumph; the boor is sent reeling.

But there is also a third and much gloomier level. Here Adams is judging the age itself. Without ever being obvious about it, he makes Carrington stand for the early days of the Republic, for the ideals of George Washington, and Ratcliffe stand for the America of party politics and big business. Madeleine herself stands for modern American consciousness of 1880—for all intelligent and idealistic Americans, asking themselves, then as now: can America function democratically in the industrial age?

On this level Ratcliffe wins hands down. Carrington may prevent him from marrying Madeleine Lee, but he cannot keep him from running the country. He cannot even hope that a change of party, or such piddling reforms as Mr. C. C. French dreams of, would make the faintest difference. At the heart of the book is a radical despair.

That in no way spoils the comedy, however. There is a lot more I haven't even mentioned, such as the story of Miss Victoria Dare, the stammering "b-b-bad girl" of Washington society and her outrageous flirtation with Lord Dunbeg. It just gives the book a kind of resonance.

And perhaps Adams's despair of American politics was not total, after all. Five years after the book came out, he made over the copyright to the National Civil Service Reform League, and for almost half a century, until long after his death, the royalties—and they were substantial—went into the effort to make democracy work. Casting a shadow, that's called.

Democracy.
Henry Adams. 1880.

15

Lords and Pagans

There are many kinds of rebels. One of the oddest and most delightful is the establishment figure who, not seeming even to notice what he's doing, subverts with his dreamy left hand all that his powerful right hand continues to uphold.

Lord Dunsany was just such a figure. The eighteenth holder of a barony created in 1439, he behaved much like any other British peer. He went to Eton. He loved fox hunting. He married an earl's daughter. He lived in a castle. He and his whole family fought for whomever happened to be the king or queen. He served in the Coldstream Guards and the Royal Inniskilling Fusiliers. His younger brother, Admiral the Hon. Sir Reginald Aylmer Ranfurly Plunkett-Ernle-Erle-Drax—a name that P. G. Wodehouse himself would hardly have dared to invent—commanded a good part of the British navy. How can you be more establishment than that?

But all the time Lord Dunsany was leading a separate fantasy life, and in that he did not uphold the established order at all. Sometimes, as in *The King of Elfland's Daughter*, he merely ignored it. And sometimes, as in *The Blessing of Pan*, he dreamily turned it on its head.

The book is laid in a quiet English village called Wolding,

80

sometime in the late nineteenth century. At first it seems to be a continuation of Anthony Trollope. The main character, you realize right away, is to be the Vicar of Wolding, a quiet man of fifty named Elderick Anwrel. As the book opens, he is just nerving himself to write a letter to his bishop. Then he does write it, causing himself to be late for tea, so that the hot buttered buns that Mrs. Tweedy the cook has made, and Marion the maid has brought in, are cold. Augusta, his wife, is mildly reproachful. Aha, you think, one of those cozy books about the gentlest of breezes in teapots that England is famous for. All that's needed is for Lord Peter Wimsey to drop in for sherry, or Mr. Pumblechook to come eat a dozen or so of the buttered buns.

How wrong you are. What Anwrel is writing his bishop about is trouble in the parish—a very strange kind of trouble. There is a big wooded hill above the village called Wold Hill, and almost every evening all spring a weirdly beautiful flute-like music has come down from the hill. There's something pagan about it. And it has such an allure that all the young girls in Wolding steal out of their houses at dark and go to the hill. They will not say what happens there.

The bishop's response to this letter is to conclude that one of his clergymen has gone bonkers. He writes back ordering Anwrel to take a two-week vacation at the shore ("the air of Brighton is particularly invigorating," his lordship writes), and in fact has his chaplain make all the arrangements. He fancies that Anwrel will come back free of these musical delusions.

Anwrel comes back to find that things are worse. He has known for some time where the music comes from; it's a young farmer's son named Tommy Duffin who is out there playing a reed pipe he made himself. But now Anwrel begins to realize what power it is that has entered Tommy. And he returns to find that now the young men of the village are stealing out at night, too.

The young men (who also know it's Tommy) had originally gone out planning to catch him, smash his pipes, and get their girls back. It didn't work out that way. Instead they fall instantly under the spell of that pagan music—and now that Tommy has all the young people of the village with him, things can begin to happen. The night the boys come is the first night that Tommy goes back behind the hill to what are known as the Old Stones of Wolding.

There are thirteen of the Old Stones: twelve standing in a circle, the thirteenth lying huge and flat in the middle. That first night, all that the boys and girls do is to dance a strange dance—somehow they know just what steps to take—in and out among the stones. But soon the music gives them a new thought. "It has an empty look, the old flat stone," one of them muses. They begin to feel they must get a bull, and perform a blood sacrifice on and for the stone.

The vicar realizes clearly that he is up against the power of the god Pan. His bishop having failed him, he turns this way and that, looking for help. He goes to a colleague in the ministry who is a great classical scholar, and so must understand Greek gods. No help there. Sturdy Protestant though he is, he goes to the reputed grave of St. Ethelbruda, who back in Saxon times is said to have driven the last pagan out of that part of England. She fails him, too.

Meanwhile, the power of the music continues to grow. Eventually, everyone in the village, to the oldest granny, is going to the Stones. Even his wife defects, as does the great lady of the neighborhood.

The climactic scene comes on a Sunday. Anwrel is preaching to a full church (his parishioners are still conventional

Victorians by day), when Tommy boldly comes right into the churchyard, playing his Panpipes. The whole congregation tiptoes out. It is that night, the night of the sun's day, that Anwrel himself defects, and it is he who sacrifices the bull at dawn on moon day, with a paleolithic stone axe. It is he, furthermore, still shepherd of the flock, who becomes leader of the pagan, nature-worshipping, low-technology community that now comes into being (and that presumably still exists) in the remote country around Wolding. That makes a powerful ending. For most of the book the reader has waited to see how Anwrel will finally defeat the forces of subversion, and it comes as a shock when he instead joins them.

This is not an antichristian book. Lord Dunsany specifically brings in St. Ethelbruda herself (there is a madman named Perkin who sees her in visions). She in heaven knows exactly what is happening in Wolding and doesn't mind a bit. To her Pan is not an enemy any longer but another of the great powers. It is just against organization, centralization, and "progress."

It is not consciously a pro-environmental book, either. Lord Dunsany could hardly have had that concept in 1928 as we now use it. He managed a pretty good prophecy of the rural counterculture though.

And finally it is not a great book. Lord Dunsany was a baron among writers as among peers, not a lofty duke. But it is a literally enchanting romance.

The Blessing of Pan.
Lord Dunsany, 1928.

16

The Best American Novel
about World War II

Great wars produce great novels. At least they do in America. The Revolution and the War of 1812, I will quickly admit, failed to, but that wasn't the fault of the wars. There wasn't anyone present to write them. In 1776, the future United States not only had no great novelists, it didn't even have a competent one. No incompetent ones, either. *England* had novelists, one of whom came over to record the Revolution, with results that appear elsewhere in this book. But not America. The situation had improved only slightly by 1812. Perhaps eight or ten people in the whole early history of our country published anything that could be called fiction, and only one of that tiny group ever became even semiprofessional.

But as soon as a true novelist did appear, and that was Fenimore Cooper in 1820, war novels commenced. Cooper's second book, *The Spy*, was a war novel (about the Revolution), and a moderately good one, too.

Every major war since then has produced at least one masterpiece. For the Civil War, it's *The Red Badge of Courage*. For World War I, *A Farewell to Arms*. As for World War II, there are numerous candidates. There are *The Naked and the Dead*, *Catch-22*, *From Here to Eternity*, maybe *The Caine Mutiny*—and then there is a book that I think will one day be recognized as better than any of these: James Gould Cozzens's *Guard of Honor*.

No one can call it a forgotten book. It has been in print continuously since its publication in 1948. People who read lists in almanacs will find it securely in the list of Pulitzer Prize winners in fiction. In its first year it was a modest best-seller, and last year it still sold seven hundred copies. Not bad.

But it *is* an underrated book by an almost sinfully under-rated author. (Cozzens did other first-class work besides *Guard of Honor.* Of his thirteen novels, three and perhaps four belong in the small but high hushed world that Melville spoke of: the world of greatness.)

I think I know why the book is so comparatively ignored. I think there are two main reasons. One involves Cozzens's personal character, and the other involves the type of novel he liked to write.

The standing of an American book tends to derive in the short run from the judgements rendered by the New York Lit-erary Establishment—which these days is only about four-fifths in New York. It now has branches in Washington and California. This loose congeries of critics, editors, writers, and probably even a few agents tends to be liberal in its po-litical and social views (which I like it for), insular and cli-quey (which I don't like it for), and deeply respectful of pub-licity (which I feel ambivalent about). Publicity conferred by itself it tends to regard as the ultimate accolade.

As for Cozzens, he tended to scorn it on all three counts. He was too dignified a man literally to stand and thumb his nose at the Establishment—but he might as well have. He did everything to outrage it. A conservative in the classic eighteenth-century sense, he was also intensely private. He did not give interviews, talk on talk shows, scratch criti-cal backs, or join movements. He acquired a reputation—

undeserved, I think—as the kind of WASP who is anti-Semitic, anti-black, and anti-urban. Except for an occasional vindictive kick, he has been largely ignored by the Establishment, and that is one reason why *Guard of Honor* does not occupy its rightful place.

In the long run, a book's standing is largely determined by professors. Professors not only write the learned books and encyclopedia entries that keep authors alive or kill them off, they pick the literature that gets taught in college. Any generation is apt to know two classes of books: the current ones favored by the Establishment and the classics selected by professors.

Guard of Honor is a classic (I think), but it is a hard one to put into an American literature course. Why? Because Cozzens was not a romantic. Most American writers, from Cooper, Poe, and Hawthorne onward, have been, and nearly all the novels in our canon are romances. This has advantages for teachers and students both. It's handy for teachers, because there is usually more to say in class about something rich in symbols and hung with cloudy portent. It is wonderful for students, because practically everyone is—and should be—a romantic at eighteen or nineteen or twenty. Clear-eyed realism comes later. Except, of course, for the considerable number of people who go directly from romanticism to disillusionment, and who thus become cynics. To them it never comes at all.

Either way, it is hard to assign books to twenty-year-olds that there is little chance they can really appreciate until they are about thirty-five, and that is another reason *Guard of Honor* does not occupy its rightful place. Hardly anyone read it in college.

Its rightful place is as one of the greatest social novels ever written in America. It's not just a slice of life, but a whole rounded pie. The action takes place at Ocanara Army Air Force Base in Florida over a three-day period in 1943. There are about twenty thousand men and women stationed at Ocanara and its satellite bases, and Cozzens seems to understand every single one of them. He has the kind of authority as author that supposedly went out with Balzac and George Eliot. (Sociology supposedly drove it out.)

The main plot concerns the apparent failure of the top officers at Ocanara—General Beal, Colonel Mowbray, Colonel Jobson—to manage so large and heterogeneous a group of people, and hence to produce an effective fighting air force. But there are dozens and even scores of subplots, not brought in one at a time, but all interwoven.

For example, there is a detachment of WACs at Ocanara, and there are something like five subplots concerned with them alone. Here is part of the story of Lieutenant Mary Lippa, a trim, athletic young woman who is both a natural commander and deeply in love with a male officer who is a natural anarchist. Part of the story of Lieutenant Amanda Turck, an intellectual almost crippled by too acute a self-consciousness and too low a self-esteem: a memorable, unhappy, and good person. Part of the history of Private Sybil Buck: rebellious and promiscuous.

For another, the air force is in the process of forming the first-ever Negro bomber group, and its planes and pilots—at this point all second lieutenants—arrive at Ocanara for training during the course of the book. Here is part of the story of Lieutenant Stanley Willis, the black flier who will eventually command that group. The whole story of a raid on the segregated officers' club by a group of the young black pilots. The effects of that on the colonel responsible for the segregation;

on Lieutenant Day, the MP stationed at the club; on Captain Wiley from Alabama, and on and on. There is material for two or three hundred movies in *Guard of Honor*, with plenty left to spare. Rarely in American fiction or in any fiction is there so fine an intermeshing of so many totally real characters. And I haven't even mentioned Captain Duchemin, the witty bon vivant who regularly gets off lines as good as any of Noel Coward's, or Lieutenant Werthauer, the medical officer who prefigures "*M*A*S*H**," or Sally Beal, the general's impetuous young wife, let alone any of the central characters.

But *Guard of Honor* is more than an account of the complex workings of a large air force base—and, by extension, of a country at war. It is two other things as well. For the reader, it is a living one's way into the military mind. The two characters through whose eyes we most often look have both fairly recently been civilians, and with them we encounter the blundering idiocy of career officers, the well-known absurdity of army regulations. But from here (which is the point at which *Catch-22* stops) we go on to understand and even to accept. Not that the military mind is right, but that there are right things about it—and, more important, that there are comprehensible reasons why it is as it is.

The second thing is closely related to the first. *Guard of Honor* makes a continuing judgement of all its characters in terms of their maturity, or capacity for achieving it. That is, the characters are divided into children and adults—a division in which Cozzens can take advantage of the military slang of that period: a commanding officer being the Old Man, a pilot a fly-boy, and so on. Some of the children are gray haired, notably Colonel Mowbray, second in command at Ocanara. Some of the adults, such as Stanley Willis, are barely out of their teens. At first the two main observers think that *all* the career military people are children, and one of the book's movements is toward their discovery that there are adults who went to West Point, or have been twenty years a noncom.

It is impossible in a short (or probably even in a long) essay to convey the subtlety with which Cozzens does all this, still less to linger on the cleverness of his minor touches, such as the way the behavior of the one actual child in the book—who is General Beal's three-year-old son—comments on the whole matter of maturity. Instead I'll just say that grownups who have not encountered *Guard of Honor* have a major treat in store. Children, including gray-haired ones, will not like it. They will find it too complex both in plot and style. Not to mention too clear eyed in its understanding of human nature. But it is fitting that, along with the Harlequins and gothics and sequels to *Peter Pan*, there be a certain number of books for grownups.

Guard of Honor.
James Gould Cozzens. 1948.

17

After Jane Austen, Who?

The Semi-Attached Couple is the answer to a good many prayers. It is the book you go on to when you have run out of Jane Austen's novels. Since Miss Austen wrote only six, people who love them run out rather quickly—and then have to wait a few years until they can read them again. Meanwhile they could be reading Miss Eden.

Emily Eden was born in 1797, one generation after Jane Austen, and one social class above her. Austen was upper middle class, the daughter of a clergyman. Eden was upper class, the daughter of Lord Auckland. She is more sentimental, more worldly, and less intelligent than Austen—but she is just as witty, and almost as delightful.

The Semi-Attached Couple was written in the 1830s, while Miss Eden was in India keeping house for her brother, the governor-general. To amuse herself on hot afternoons in Calcutta, she began to write a novel about love and politics among the English nobility. These were subjects she understood well. Her sister Eleanor had been the one great love of William Pitt, the earl's son who became prime minister of England at twenty-four. Eleanor later became countess of Buckinghamshire. She herself had a romantic attachment to the eldest son of another prime minister. The affair ended badly, and she had to go to France to recover. Loves like these appear constantly in *The Semi-Attached Couple*, but transformed, so that everything ends happily.

The book has a huge cast of characters. At the center are the semi-attached couple themselves: Lady Helen Beaufort, age eighteen, and her brand-new husband, the marquess of Teviot. They are semi-attached because Lady Helen really wasn't ready to get married. She was swept off her feet by one of the greatest noblemen in England, and she quickly discovers that she would much rather be back in Eskdale Castle with her large and loving family. *They* are not always breathing passion, having fits of jealousy, turning icy with Byronic pride. The central plot of the book is Lady Helen's eventually falling in love with her own husband.

Around these two swirl dozens of other people. Lady Portmore, the heartless society flirt is there, trying to break marriages up, and especially Lord Teviot's. M. La Grange, the Anglophile Frenchman is there, making jokes in a heavy accent and madly taking notes for the book he intends to write when he gets back to Paris. There are at least three other romances, two of which could be straight out of *Pride and Prejudice*. There is also a splendid parliamentary election.

What makes the book such a delight is a combination of two things: Miss Eden's steady flow of ironic wit, and her very unironic view of how nice it is to be young, rich, and handsome—as so many people in the book are. (She has no doubts about the joys of being nobly born, either.) For example, just before the Teviot wedding, two upper-middle-class sisters named Sarah and Eliza Douglas are getting a look at Lady Helen's trousseau.

"'Thirty morning gowns!' whispered Sarah as they went downstairs. "The idea of a new gown every day for a month! Now I call that real happiness.'"

Or their mother's comment, much later in the book, when her husband gets to talking politics—in this case the politics of Spain and Portugal, troubled then as now.

"'No, my dear Mr. Douglas, don't go off on those tiresome foreign affairs. What can it signify which conquers which, or who dethrones who, at that distance? Let them fight it out quietly. Besides, you need not pretend to understand national feuds if you have not found out what is passing under your eyes; but I cannot believe it, you must see what an unhappy couple these poor Teviots are!'"

One could assemble fifty good quotes from Mrs. Douglas alone.

The book has its flaws, of course. With one or two exceptions like Colonel Ernest Beaufort (age twenty-six, and a London dandy), Miss Eden does not draw male characters nearly as well as female ones. She has a habit, from which Jane Austen is quite free, of quoting bad romantic poetry at intense moments. But I will nonetheless confidently predict that almost anyone who picks the book up will find himself or herself instantly drawn in, and on finishing it will be looking hopefully around for more. Should that happen to you, I have good news. Miss Eden wrote a second novel, almost as good, called *The Semi-Detached House*.

The Semi-Attached Couple.
Emily Eden. 1860.

18

America's Greatest Diarist

A century and a half ago, when New York was a minicity of 250,000 people, and Columbia University was a mini-college with barely a hundred students, a boy named George Templeton Strong graduated at the age of eighteen, and immediately began the study of law. At twenty-one he entered practice with his father's Wall Street firm. Soon he plunged headlong into the life of the city. At twenty-seven he became a vestryman of Trinity Church, at thirty-three a trustee of Columbia. At thirty-six he helped to found the Columbia Law School. At forty he found himself placed (to his astonishment) on an all-male committee that was to decide who was "in" society and who was out.

At forty-one he all but laid aside his law practice for four years to work for the great Sanitary Commission that saved so many soldiers' lives during the Civil War. At forty-four he declined the presidency of Columbia. At fifty he became president of the New York Philharmonic Society. Meanwhile, he had married and raised a family, been to almost every fire in the city, attended all the concerts, heard all the gossip, followed all the elections, been interested in pretty much everything that happened in this country in his time.

He had meanwhile kept a four-million word diary. It begins when he is fifteen and ends only with his death in 1875. It is full of nuggets, delights, and gems. Through it one can track the growth of all sorts of things in America. Technology, for example. The industrial revolution took shape in his time, and Strong followed it with fascination. Back in 1836, when he was only sixteen, an older relative took him on board one of the big new steamboats then beginning to appear in eastern ports. "She is a superb boat, and has *baths* on board, which is quite a novel arrangement," he wrote admiringly in his diary.

He watched the growth of factories—and aristocrat though he was, felt furious most of his life at the working conditions in them. When a big and shoddily built one in Massachusetts collapsed, killing many of the women and girls who worked in it, Strong quite seriously would have liked to see the owner hanged: "Somebody has murdered about two hundred people, many of them with hideous torture, in order to save money, but society has no gibbet for the respectable millionaire."

He rode on the new railroads, admired a piece of the new metal called aluminum that a friend showed him, cast his vote in one of the new glass ballot boxes that were part of the (vain) attempt to reform city politics. ("They say that the price of a councilman is from $10 to $25," he noted angrily on December 29, 1854. He means, of course, for a vote on any one particular bill. Even then, it cost a lot more to buy one full time.) And all these things he recorded.

That's only the public side of his diary. Ample as that is, it pales before the private side. Strong gives a really stunning evocation of what it was like to be a city dweller back in the days of our national innocence. It was rather different than most people imagine. For example, it was less quiet than I had supposed. Probably from a series of English movies, and maybe a few Currier & Ives prints, I had thought nineteenth-century city sounds were mostly the clip-clop of horses' hooves and a few picturesque street-sellers' cries. Not so. Here is an entry Strong made on June 15, 1845. He was living in his father's big brick house on Greenwich Street.

This being Sunday night, our neighbors in the rear are comparatively quiet—there's only the average choir of cats, a pulmonary horse (stabled within 25 feet of this room), afflicted with a periodic cough of great severity at regular intervals of about 15 minutes, and a few drunken Dutch emigrants singing what I've no doubt's a highly indecent Low Dutch canticle, fortunately unintelligible. . . . It's quite a Sabbath stillness; for on an ordinary evening, there are two Dutch lust-houses in Washington Street that keep an orchestra apiece.

Some stillness.

Or he'll note in 1857 that there's such a crime wave that most of his friends have bought revolvers, and carry them. (A gang called the Dead Rabbits was behind a lot of the trouble.) And he decides that if he had to be out on foot after dark much, he'd do the same, "though it's a very bad practice carrying concealed weapons."

More personally still, you learn of Strong's numerous experiments with drugs. He doesn't take opium, though there was plenty in the city ("much more than people think"); it was that new drug chloroform that he loved to trip with. "It seems an innocent kind of amusement, not followed by any reaction or other unpleasant symptoms," he coolly writes when he is twenty-eight—and then records his latest trip in full detail. (Among other things, he hallucinated a performance of Mozart's Requiem, with "accompaniment by an orchestra and, as I noticed at the time, not a very good one.") Eight years later he is still enjoying periodic chloroform binges.

Most personal of all, you get his feelings as he meets,

courts, and marries Miss Ellen Ruggles. There is an especially touching dialogue he holds with himself two weeks before the wedding. His romantic self says to him that he's going to worship her forever. His commonsensical self presumes to doubt. "Don't you know that five years hence or ten years hence your Wife will be an everyday affair and not the lovely novelty that she is now?" And he makes himself a solemn promise never to *act* as if she were everyday. (He mostly kept it, too.)

But there is really a record of almost everything in this book. You want to know when flowers began commonly to appear on altars in Protestant churches in New York? In 1856. "Censured as papistical, of course." Want to know the state of mathematics in American colleges five generations ago? Well, granted that Columbia happened to be in especially bad shape, scientifically, in the 1850s, here's something of an eye opener. The physics professor had complained that the math professor was incompetent (true), and that students were coming to him unprepared. Strong, that master of detail, records some of the problems Columbia juniors couldn't handle in 1857. They couldn't compute the interest on $1,000 for sixty days at 7 percent; they couldn't say how much three-fourths of five-fifths came to; they couldn't prove the Pythagorean theorem. Educational standards in 1988 may be less disastrous than people fear.

Strong already had a solution in mind, incidentally, for keeping professors on their toes. He'd heard it from Professor Peirce of Harvard. You should just require them "to accomplish something every year or every six months . . . some essay, memoir, or investigation."

Just so I won't seem to be picking on Columbia, want to know how Yale struck an elegant New Yorker in 1846?

As piddling and provincial. After sneering at the buildings, Strong notes the social life of the faculty. He went to "Mrs. Salisbury's big dinner party—very magnificent affair— *no wine.*"

Strong also records hundreds of cultural events, and here the note is usually one of joy. Our symphonic warhorses were to him contemporary music. Like Barbellion, he particularly loved what we call Beethoven's Fifth and he called the C Minor Symphony. The Strongs heard a performance on September 29, 1853. "That noblest of compositions was never so played in this city before. Ellie was cured of a cold by it."

There are some less pleasing entries, of course. Like most people of his time and class, Strong was a good deal of a bigot. He didn't think much of Irish immigrants, and he thought even less of blacks. (Though he was capable of change. His slow and reluctant conversion to antislavery feeling makes a fascinating case study. The first glimmerings appear in 1854. Actual dawn was in 1856, when Congressman Preston Brooks of South Carolina clubbed Senator Charles Sumner of Massachusetts in the Senate chamber for speaking too virulently against slavery. "The reckless, insolent brutality of our Southern aristocrats may drive me into abolitionism yet," Strong wrote. By 1860 he was voting for Lincoln.)

In any case, Strong's sharp tongue was by no means reserved for blacks and immigrants. He could be devastating on his fellow WASPs. Here is his description of that reverend old gentleman Peter Cooper, founder of the Cooper Union. The Prince of Wales is visiting New York; Strong is on the committee to receive him. He is watching his fellow New Yorkers surge in to the reception, eager to clasp the hand of royalty. Among those who catch his attention are "old Pelatiah Perit (who looked like a duke in his dress coat and white cravat) and Peter Cooper, who looked like one of Gulliver's Yahoos caught and cleaned and dressed up."

Or consider what he had to say about John Tyler at a time when that gentleman was fifty-four years old and president of the United States. (Strong is twenty-four.) He has just heard that the president has married again—"one of those large fleshy Miss Gardiners of Gardiner's Island." Strong does not respectfully salute the Chief Magistrate, and wish him felicitations. "Poor, unfortunate, deluded old jackass," he writes. "It's positively painful to think of his situation, and the trials that lie before him."

The fact is that most good diarists have a touch of acerbity. But the great ones—and Strong is of their number—have something more. Or, to be accurate, one of two things. They have either a self-absorbtion so intense and so pure that it transcends both self and selfishness. Anne Frank is an example. Or they have an inexhaustible love of the world they live in. Pepys is of this kind. So is George Templeton Strong. In 1855, a few months before Whitman brought out the first obscure edition of *Leaves of Grass*, Strong made an entry which expresses that embracing love. It is worth quoting at length. He has been thinking about American poets and wishing they would leave the Middle Ages and Helen of Troy alone. Let them look homeward.

There is poetry enough latent in the South Street merchant and the Wall Street financier; in Stewart's snobby clerk chaffering over ribbons and laces; in the omnibus driver that conveys them all . . . in the sumptuous courtesan of Mercer Street thinking sadly of her village home; in the Fifth Avenue ballroom; in the Grace Church contrast of eternal vanity and new bonnets; in the dancers at Lewis Jones and Mr. Schiff's, and in the future of each and all.

Nice words, those. Strong is, in fact, a kind of upper-class Whitman—a fact he almost certainly didn't know, since he seems never to have read or met Walt.

There is one last thing to add. Quoting especially good passages as I have been, I may have given the impression that the whole four volumes of this diary are worth reading. They aren't. At least not word for word. The first few years are the precocious pedantic writing of a book-mad youth. It is only in his middle twenties that Strong really finds his style. And even after that, there is more about the politics of the Episcopal Church and the doings of Columbia College than most people are going to want to hear. But every page of the whole two thousand is worth skimming, and there are long sections that deserve full attention.

As usual, Strong himself has the last word. He possessed a lively sense of futurity. (He loved to imagine what New York would be like a hundred or even a thousand years after his time.) Once, as a young man, he imagined his descendants in the far-off twentieth century thumbing through the diary. They would find it, he decided, "a queer old journal . . . that nobody could read through, but which contains curious illustrations of old times."

Curious, wonderful, and intensely real.

The Diary of George Templeton Strong.
Ed. Allan Nevins and Milton Thomas. 1952.

19

The Night-and-Fog People

Sometimes human beings are hard to like. We are selfish, cruel, and greedy. We foul the earth. We exterminate other species. (We've got tigers down to about four thousand, meanwhile increasing our own numbers more than that every hour.) We are full of self-pity.

In an anti-heroic age such as the present, any sense of human niceness is especially hard to come by. Our literature is devoted to deriding concepts like courage and self-sacrifice; our biographers specialize in revealing that persons previously thought to be heroes had feet, ankles, and even thighs of clay—and were probably hollow, to boot. Depressing.

Henriette Roosenburg's *The Walls Came Tumbling Down* is a splendid antidote to all this. Here is a book full of utterly unselfconscious heroism. Here is an author who shows in the most matter-of-fact way just how generous and brave human beings can be. She even shows, without particularly meaning to, that patriotism can be a solemn and lofty thing—it may be the last refuge of scoundrels, but under the right circumstances it is also the first thought of heroes. Best of all, her story is both true and well told.

Henriette Roosenburg, a middle-class Dutch girl with a fondness for literature, was a graduate student at the Unviersity of Leiden when World War II came along. She became a courier in the Dutch resistance movement, code name Zip. In 1944, she was caught and condemned to death.

But the Nazis didn't immediately execute everyone they sentenced. Some they kept as prisoners, for possible killing later. Such prisoners were in a sense officially dead already, and they were universally known as the *Nacht und Nebel* or Night and Fog people. NNs formed the lowest class of prisoners to be found in German jails and camps. The top class was German criminals—your ordinary murderer or thief. Then came black marketeers and other criminals from the occupied countries. Third were political prisoners, "ranging from the unfortunate innocent who had been denounced for listening to the BBC to the active resistance member who had been caught in an act of sabotage, of distributing an illegal newspaper, of sheltering Jews," or any other forbidden thing. The politicals were harshly treated, but they did have some rights, such as the right to go on sick call.

Finally came the *Nacht und Nebelen*, with no rights at all. Whenever enough cells were available, they were kept in solitary confinement. They got no mail, no medical attention, few amenities (Zip was allowed to bathe three times in eight months), very little food.

But Zip is not writing a book about her sufferings in prison, any more than she is about her heroism in the underground. (Her entire description of her job before she was caught is to mention casually that she transmitted information about German troop movements to London "and occasionally helped Allied pilots when they happened to get stuck.") This is a book about what happened after the war ended, and it is profoundly moving.

When the war ended, Zip was in prison in the little Saxon town of Waldheim. Like other NNs, she existed on a slice of bread in the morning, a bowl of thin soup at noon, a slice of bread and an ounce of cottage cheese or ersatz jam in the evening. Plus every couple of weeks a few potatoes.

To be a little more cruel, the prison guards in Waldheim gave out both slices of bread in the evening. By bitter experience, the prisoners learned that they had to save one of the two slices overnight, or next morning's hunger pangs were simply unendurable. Not easy to save a slice of bread for twelve hours when you're starving.

It was the Russians who freed her. Their army came into Waldheim on May 6, 1945. At that time there were thirty-two surviving female NNs in the prison, a small number of male NNs, and many hundreds of politicals and ordinary criminals.

In keeping with their nonstatus, the female NNs were in the most obscure part of the women's wing. When Russian soldiers came and began unlocking the cells, they did not unlock the NN cells. They did not know about them. Others surged out; the NNs banged vainly on their doors. "The noise in the prison swelled to a mighty roar, wave following wave, around us, near us, and yet not near enough."

This moment is when the human spirit begins to shine. Just as they are in despair, there was "a rush of wooden sandals on the staircase and shrill French voices shouting, 'Les condamnés à mort, les condamnés à mort!' The French politicals had not forgotten us; they were coming to our rescue."

Soon the NNs are out in the corridor—and like every other starved prisoner in Waldheim, they are tottering toward where they think the kitchens must be. At that moment the lights go out, and in the darkness pandemonium begins. There could have been a scene of mass trampling as the prisoners, "mad with the first taste of freedom" and really almost crazed with hunger, fought on toward the kitchens.

But at this moment one of the French politicals began to sing the *Marseillaise*. Henriette Roosenburg writes, "I have always loved the *Marseillaise*, and if ever I wanted to sing it, this was the moment. Yet I kept respectfully silent, for at the moment I felt they had an exclusive right to it."

Then, jammed there together in the dark, these starving people sang their national songs one by one: the Poles, the Czechs, the Belgians, the handful of Dutch. "It was the most solemn moment in my life, barring none. It was also the best thing that could have happened psychologically. It pulled us together, changed us from hungry animals into human beings with a purpose and a pride. The old spirit of the resistance, dulled and deadened by endless months of starvation and dehumanization, came alive again; the pushing and pulling stopped and we were courteous to one another. In the darkness a hand came across and pushed a slice of bread into my hand. I said, 'No, no, keep it,' and a voice next to me whispered, 'No, it's yours, I stole it from your blanket, I'm sorry.' I took the bread and started eating it."

Once the lights come back, the prisoners make their way in moderate order to the kitchens, which they find the German criminals who did the cooking have fortified. (There is not a guard in sight.) Ignoring a dozen or so Russian soldiers who are lying on the floor copulating with some of the well-fed women from the two upper classes of prisoners, the politicals and the NNs pry loose a good deal of food and then set about organizing themselves into national groups, making flags, and thinking about how they will get home.

From that point of view, it is very bad luck for the western Europeans that the Russians got there first. The Russians are going to let no one through their lines. The Czechs and Poles don't have to cross, and over the next week most of them are able to leave for home, as they gradually recover the strength to walk. But the westerners are stuck. The rumor is that the Russians will herd them into a camp, ship them to Odessa, and then decide what to do. Meanwhile, they continue living in the prison.

The Dutch group is tiny. It consists of four women and one man, a young merchant seaman named Dries. (*He* was condemend to death for attempting to get to England in a small boat in 1944.)

One of the four women, Fafa, is crippled with arthritis, unable even to stand up. She has had, of course, no treatment of any kind, not even an aspirin to ease the pain. It is because of her that the next piece of heroism arises.

On the sixth day of their freedom, a miracle occurs. An American army convoy of six trucks rumbles into Waldheim. Word has reached the west of the prisoners here, and quite illegally the convoy has come to get them. The Russians occasionally wink at the no-crossing-the-lines rule for fellow soldiers.

There are more western prisoners than there is room in the trucks—even though you can get a lot of eighty- and ninety-pound adults onto one truck. But Zip and her friends found the trucks early. They could easily have gotten on. There is no possible room for Fafa, however, nor could she have endured the ride over the shattered roads in any case. Right now she is lying in one of the remote NN cells—there is not even any way to carry her out of the prison. They will not abandon her to probable death. All five Dutch stay behind, knowing it may mean months or years in Odessa.

In the rest of the book, Henriette Roosenburg tells how they got Fafa safely placed in a civilian hospital run by an icy but honorable Prussian doctor and how the other four then set out to evade the Russians and get home. Many books are

called odysseys; this one truly is, even in the literal sense
that it's a trip by water. Holland is a country of canals and
rivers, and it came naturally to these four young Dutch people
to head for the river Elbe, where they hope to steal a boat.
(Their finding two Dutch barges trapped on the Elbe by broken
bridges, and their reception by the skippers of those two
barges brought tears to my eyes, I suppose for the fourth or
fifth time. It's *nice* to feel proud of human beings.)

But there are more than tearful scenes in this book. There's
everything. There are scenes where Zip and the others have
their chance at revenge on the prison guards, and do or don't
take it. There are scenes with the Russians that make you
both love and get furiously exasperated with that mercurial
people. There's even humor, such as the scene in a German
house where they have pushed their way in to spend the
night. One woman in the house, herself a half-crazed refugee
from Allied bombing, can't rest until she finds out which of
the three young women Dries is sleeping with. The answer is
none, in the sense that she means it. They have been too
terribly starved. "None of us girls had menstruated for six
months; Dries, after the first two nights of cuddling up close
for lack of space, had confided that we didn't have to worry
because, much as he loved the atmosphere, he couldn't have
an erection."

But that answer would be unacceptable to the romantic
housewife.

"All right, Zip," said Dries resignedly, "let's be married for
one night, but let's tuck the girls in first."

When the book ends, Zip is home, and she is giving her
mother as a present the one personal possession she had in
prison; a six-inch square cut from her own underpants on
which she had painstakingly embroidered a miniature history

of her whole captivity. (Many of the NNs who survived kept their sanity with secret and illegal embroidery—and there were times when a starving man would trade a scrap of his tiny food allowance for six inches of a particular color of thread.) Zip's mother collapses in tears. "You couldn't have done this," she sobs, "you never even knew in which hand to hold a needle."

This is a book that makes you realize human beings can do practically anything. And it makes you glad we exist, glad the universe contains such creatures.

The Walls Came Tumbling Down.
Henriette Roosenburg. 1957.

20

Irreverence in the Year 1239

In the year 1239, Manuel the high count of Poictesme disappeared from his realm, never to return. Since his only son was a child of two, rule passed to his wife, the young Countess Niafer. For the next nineteen years she governed Poictesme, partly according to her own ideas, partly to suit her principal adviser, a Christian saint and missionary known as Holy Holmendis.

One result of Count Manuel's disappearance was the breakup of the military order of which he had been the founder and leader: the Fellowship of the Silver Stallion. The members, besides himself, had been the nine barons of Poictesme, who included such notable warriors as Kerin of Nointel, Donander of Évre, and that great magician Miramon Lluagor. One by one most of these barons also left Poictesme, some to follow other leaders in other wars, some in search of Count Manuel, one to abandon knightly adventures and become a scholar. By 1260, all but two had gone.

Is this some obscure scrap of European history? No, it's the imagined background for a very curious novel. James Branch Cabell is one of the long line of sword-and-sorcery writers that runs from Sir Thomas Malory down to yesterday's pulp fantasist, and he is like no other on the list. An extreme ro-

mantic, he is simultaneously an extreme sceptic. A writer
elegant and learned far beyond the American norm, he is also
fond of smut. A lover of courtly good manners, he nevertheless delights in truly breathtaking irreverence.

The Silver Stallion is cast in the form of medieval chron-
icle. The book opens at Count Manuel's castle soon after his
disappearance. His nine barons have gathered publicly for
the formal disbanding of the order and privately to discuss
what to do with the rest of their lives, now that the young
countess and Saint Holmendis have set about reforming Poictesme into dull piety. Mostly they decide to avoid the new regime by becoming knights errant. Cabell then follows them
one by one on their adventures.

Lord Gonfal of Naimes is the first to leave. He journeys
south, to the land of Inis Dahut, where a quest has been cried
for the hand of dark-haired Queen Morvyth. In the best fairy-
tale style, the suitor who is to win her must fare forth, do
battle with evil, and return in a year with some splendid prize
to be his bridal gift. Best prize gets queen.

Eight candidates appear: seven youthful princes, and Lord
Gonfal, who seems to be in his late thirties. There is a fine
scene as the eight draw their swords and swear fealty to the
quest. At that moment the tale veers off to become Cabellian. As the eight resheathe their shining blades, one clumsy
fellow drops his, and it pierces his own left foot. That fellow
is Lord Gonfal, who is thus compelled to stay in Inis Dahut
and recuperate, while the seven princes go a-questing.

By the time they return, each with a noble treasure, Gonfal
and the queen are old friends. So close have they become that
she is reluctant to pick the winning treasure and marry the
hero who brought it. These princelings no longer interest her.
She says openly that she rather wishes the various dragons
and giants had killed them, rather than vice versa.

There was never a chance. "'Each of these men is the shrewd, small and ill-favoured third son of a king [Gonfal tells her]. It is the law that such unprepossessing midgets should prosper, and override every sort of evil, in the Isles of Wonder and all other extra-mundane lands.'"

"'But is it fair, my friend [the queen persists] is it even respectful, to the august and venerable powers of iniquity, that these whippersnappers—?'"

The upshot is that she decides none of the treasures they brought are worthy, and renews the quest for a second year. Gonfal's foot has long since healed, and he is to go too. Once again eight swords are drawn for a solemn vow. But just as the eight champions, bearing their bright blades, are ascending the steps of the altar of Pygé-Upsizugos to be blessed by the high priest, one slips on the polished stone steps. It's Gonfal again. His sword flies out of his hand. Quickly he catches it—and, lo, the keen edge has cut through bone and tendon of his right hand. Once again he is compelled to tarry at court. Next year . . . but you'll have to read Cabell for that.

The next to leave is Lord Coth, the stubbornest and most bull-necked of the nine barons. He journeys west, searching for his liege lord. After many adventures he comes to a far empire called Porutsa. There, just outside the capital city, he comes on a vast black statue in a field of wild green peppers. Obviously it's the local deity, and judging by the numbers of human bones lying about, this is his place of sacrifice.

As a matter of mere civility, Coth kneels and offers homage to the statue. To his considerable surprise, it is promptly accepted. The god appears in person, huge and naked. His name is Yaotl. Within minutes he is giving blessings to his new worshipper (Coth is to be the next emperor of Porutsa, Yaotl decrees) and also putting commandments on him. Among these are the command to refrain from public nudity—this is a privilege of divinity—and to respect the sacred green peppers. Yaotl then departs.

Coth hates being told what to do. He instantly strips off his clothes, gathers all the peppers he can carry, and heads into town. There he is arrested and taken before the current emperor for questioning, "Who are you, and what is your business in Porutsa?" the emperor asks.

Coth is much too busy disobeying Yaotl's commandments to explain his real mission. "I am an outlander called Coth of the Rocks, a dealer in green peppers, and I came hither to sell my green peppers," he says coolly. Naturally all this infuriates Yaotl (though it enchants the emperor's daughter, who has never seen a pink, naked outlander before). In the end, Coth suffers a still stranger fate than Gonfal's.

But my favorite of the adventures is that which happens to Donander of Évre. As Coth was the stubbornest of Count Manuel's barons, Donander is the stupidest. He is an exceptionally good soldier, but not quick of thought. When Donander leaves Poictesme, he joins a Christian army that is crusading against the pagan Norsemen. When Red Palnatoki, the Norse champion, issues a challenge, it is Donander who comes clanking out in full armor to meet him. Their swordplay is astounding and ceases only when the heroes have mortally wounded each other. Then the tale becomes Cabellian.

The fight has been witnessed not only by the two armies, but by two divine messengers. One is the angel Ithuriel, the other a sort of male Valkyrie named Kjalar. They are present to gather up those who die fighting bravely and to take them, respectively, to heaven and to Valhalla. They have been doing this sort of thing almost daily for centuries and are old friends. Chatting away as the fight goes on, they get careless. Each takes the wrong soul, so that Palnatoki winds up in heaven and Donander in Valhalla. It would be hard to say which is funnier, Palnatoki's subsequent involvement with the Great Whore of Babylon (the only woman in heaven he finds even faintly interesting), or Donander's inability to grasp just where and what he is. He continues to worship at a small Christian shrine he has set up, eons after he has become a Norse god himself.

Cabell is not everyone's dish of tea. The sexual innuendo that seemed so daring in 1926 is not going to give nearly so many little delightful shocks and thrills now. His vast impudence is going to amuse younger readers more than older ones—it amused *me* more when I was twenty than it does now. (I was more interested in seeing authority figures successfully mocked in those days.) His smooth and elaborate style will not impress admirers of minimalism; it may even annoy them.

But there truly is tea in the cup: a smoky and sophisticated Lapsang souchong. People who delight in polish and poise and wit, who like to see an absolute master of invention, will like *The Silver Stallion.*

The Silver Stallion.
James Branch Cabell. 1926.

21

A Tale of Many Virtues

Junk food and junk books have a number of things in common. One is that both are perceived in a state of isolation. There is real food, which provides some kind of health or nutritional benefit. And there is junk food, which doesn't. It exists in its own squalid ghetto of instant gratification.

Similarly, there are real books, which have vision, or something to say, or redeeming social value. And there are junk books, which don't. They are quite separate. A junk book is not an unusually bad collection of poems, or a wretchedly edited encyclopedia. It is a book *designed* as trash: a bunch of lists, a piece of porn, some squalid rented daydream.

But on closer examination, both kinds of junk turn out to have noble cousins. Junk food, for example, is a machine full of candy bars, or a shelf of little packaged "cakes," most of them injected with some kind of filling. The filling, mostly coconut oil and fierce preservatives, is a horrible parody of whipped cream. Dreadful! And yet behind this junk looms the noble chocolate of Tobler, the dessert cart of a great restaurant, the *madeleines* of Marcel Proust. And one has no need to despise the cream puffs at Les Pointes because Drake's Cakes exist.

Similarly with junk books. They are most commonly romantic novels. Absurdly erotic if for men, ludicrously unrealistic (especially as to the heroes) if for women. Full of

exotic backgrounds, poorly imagined. Tinsel! And yet behind
this junk rise up a whole range of splendid romances, and
even a few actual great works, like *Jane Eyre*.

The Maker of Heavenly Trousers is not a great work, but it's
a splendid romance. It's erotic, exotic and unrealistic—and
it's all of these things with style and dash. Even with substance. It's the sort of book a Harlequin would be if it could.

I'll start with the exotic. The setting could hardly be more
so. The book opens in Peking in the last days of the Ch'ing
dynasty. That is, around 1908. In the Inner City, far from the
foreign quarter, there is a "house" consisting of many court-
yards and pavilions. Once it was a Manchu temple called the
Shuang Liè Ssè. Now it's the private residence of a wealthy
foreigner who chooses to live in native style. Its current name
is the Home of the Five Virtues: not because this foreigner is
some paragon of Confucian morality, but because his five
principal servants all are related, and all have the family
name of Tò. Tò means virtue. Tò-tai, or Exalted Virtue, is the
major-domo; Tò-shan, or Mountain of Virtue, does the gardening, and so on. The servants, the house, the historic
marble lions out front, the tailor up the street who makes
those heavenly trousers, all this is richly exotic. Accurate,
too. The book is worth reading simply as the portrait of a marvelous time and place. (I'd give anything to have just one pair
of socks darned by Exalted Virtue's wife. Instead of neat
patches over the holes, embroidered scarlet bats.)

But it is also worth reading on much lower grounds. Let me
turn to the erotic, of which there is considerable.

The central plot of the book concerns the wealthy foreigner
(who narrates the story and whose name we never learn) and
his interest in a girl called Kuniang. When you first meet her,
she is twelve years old and she is playing in one of the court-

yards with Little Lu, Exalted Virtue's son. She is not Chinese. Kuniang ("Girl") is simply what the Virtues call her. Her father is Italian, Signor Cante de' Tolomei, of a once-great Sienese family. Her mother, a Scandinavian, is dead. While the mother lived, the de' Tolomeis had a nearby apartment and were one of the three European families in that whole quarter of Peking.

The narrator—who is young as well as rich—gives orphaned Kuniang one of the pavilions to live in, and the Five Virtues raise her. She grows into a beautiful young woman. Naturally she plays less and less with Little Lu (seven years her junior), or with Fédor and Natasha, the two Russian children down the street, and spends more and more time with the narrator. At sixteen she begins to take her meals at his table. Finally, when she is nineteen and he is thirty-four, passion enters their lives. It does so in a way that girls whose amorous experience is chiefly in parked cars might envy.

The narrator has an almost unrivaled collection of Chinese silks. Among them is a great cloak of rose-colored satin, once owned by an emperor. It was used by palace eunuchs to wrap a chosen concubine (who is otherwise quite naked) and carry her to the imperial bedroom. Kuniang (who always sleeps naked) is thus carried from her pavilion to the narrator's. She enjoys the trip. "I always thought it would be much more fun to be a concubine," she says happily. Later, though she considers such ceremonies a bit silly, she does agree to get married.

Kuniang is too young and innocent to carry the whole weight of the book. She doesn't have to. There is also Elisalex, alias the Princess Dorbon Oirad. (That's a Mongolian title, in case you're wondering, though Elisalex herself is Russian.)

Elisalex turns up in Peking because she has been expelled from Russia following the murder of Rasputin in 1916. She was his mistress, following her marriage to Prince Dorbon. She is twenty-five, nobly born (Fedor's grandfather was one of her grandfather's serfs), a woman even more fearless than beautiful. And more reckless even than brave. Much as I'd like to have a pair of socks darned with scarlet bats, I'd like still more to have met Elisalex and shared her adventures in Mongolia and in the palace of Duke Lan. Even to know her in a book is much.

As to lack of realism, there is some of that too. Obviously I shan't praise it in the way I have the exoticism and eroticism. Instead I shall quickly note that there are one or two excessive improbabilities, such as the strange birthmark shared by Kuniang and Elisalex and such as the psychic powers of Prince Dorbon, and then pass on to the book's final charm.

Like a confection at Rumpemayer's, it is made of the finest ingredients. Romances are usually written by people with more imagination than culture. Hence the tinsel effect. But Daniele Varé was a man quite as extraordinary as his characters. Like Elisalex, he came of a great family. His was Venetian. Like the narrator and Kuniang, he knew China from the inside. Signor Varé was first secretary in the Italian embassy in Peking from 1912 to 1920—and then came back in 1927 as the ambassador from Italy. He went everywhere. Besides his novels, he wrote a biography of the last Ch'ing empress, and dozens of essays on Chinese history. Besides Chinese, Italian, French, and German, he spoke English so flawlessly that it was his amusement to compose some of his books in our language. *The Maker of Heavenly Trousers* is such a one. What I've been describing is the original. It's Italians reading

Il creatore di celesti pantaloni who get a translation foisted upon them.

There is no redeeming social value whatsoever to the stories of Kuniang and Elisalex. But they form one of the most delightful daydreams you could possibly rent.

The Maker of Heavenly Trousers.
Daniele Varé. 1935.

22

Sailing to London

What with the lofty language of *Moby-Dick* and Conrad's *Lord Jim* and John Masefield's sea poems, not to mention varous real-life phenomena such as China clippers and Columbus and Joshua Slocum sailing alone around the world, and of course there's the *Mayflower* too, we are used to thinking of sailing ships in the heroic mode. Nor are we wrong: for seamen it *was* a sterner age than our present era of cruise ships and tankers with air-conditioned crew quarters.

But it wasn't all white whales and perilous voyages either. There was also plenty of humdrum sailing. Up until about a hundred years ago, for example, garbage was taken out into Chesapeake Bay in sailing barges, and cargoes of beer and cowhides went up and down the coast in dirty little schooners that hugged the shore.

It is this kind of seafaring, in its English version, that W. W. Jacobs writes about in *Many Cargoes*. Like that of his younger contemporary P. G. Wodehouse, his mode is comedy tinged with romance. But where Wodehouse cast an amused, affectionate eye on the aristocracy, and found the rest of England all but invisible, Jacobs directs a similar gaze on the small bourgeoisie and the working classes. The characters in his stories are the captains, mates, and crews of coastal ships sailing from tiny English ports to London and back again. A typical voyage might be three days. A typical captain might own his little ship, employ one mate and a crew of four. He might also have his wife or daughter along.

This unheroic but still nautical life yields, in Jacobs's deft hands, an almost infinite quantity of humor. The very first story in *Many Cargoes* is a classic and a gem. It's set on a relatively large if unglamorous ship ("as slow an old tub as ever I was aboard of," says the narrator) with two mates and a crew of eight. There is also the captain, who doubles as ship's doctor. Nothing special about that—very few merchantmen carried trained physicians, even barques like this, which might be at sea for several weeks. But the captain doesn't just have a little kit, he is deeply interested in medicine and fancies himself a keen diagnostician.

At first you hear about him from the point of view of the two mates, who merely complain of the scalpels he keeps in the cabin and of his habit of making them take pills of his own composition whenever he thinks they need toning up.

Then the scene shifts to the fo'c'sle, where the eight sailors live. "'One day,'" the narrator says, "'I seed old Dan'l Dennis sitting on a locker reading. Every now and then he'd shut the book, an' look up, closing 'is eyes, an' moving his lips like a hen drinking, an' then look down at the book again.

"'Why, Dan,' I ses, 'what's up? you ain't larning lessons at your time o' life?'

"'Yes, I am,' ses Dan very soft. 'You might hear me say it, it's this one about heart disease.'"

Then he recites the symptoms he has just learned from the book, which turns out to be one of those home health-care manuals, groans a little, and asks the narrator to go fetch the captain.

"'I see his little game,'" the narrator continues, "'but I wasn't going to run any risks, so I just mentioned, permiscous like, to the cook as old Dan seemed rather queer, an' went back an' tried to borrer the book, being always fond of reading.'" No luck. "'Old Dan pretended he was too ill to hear what I was saying, an' afore I could take it away from him, the skipper comes hurrying down with a bag in his 'and.'"

Dan recites his symptoms, and the skipper listens in mounting excitement as one by one they build to the descriptions of heart disease in *his* books. He confines Dan to his bunk and prescribes a special diet full of delicacies like beef tea. There arc now seven left to sail the ship.

Within an hour, a seaman called Cornish Harry, a large, brutal man, takes the book away from Dan by main force and proceeds to come down with consumption. Now six sailors are doing the work.

After two days of that, some of the others demand that Harry and Dan get well and let them have turns lying in bed all day being nursed on beef tea.

"'*Well?*' ses Harry, '*well?* Why you silly iggernerant chaps, we shan't never get well, people with our complaints never do.'"

Eventually, two more of the crew, those who are least afraid of Harry, get sick. Now there are four left to sail the ship. At this point the first mate, who has never been fooled for a minute, but who of course must obey his captain, comes up with a daring plan, based on a truly vile medicine that he concocts in the ship's galley and that he pretends he learned about from his grandmother. The captain reluctantly lets him give the four invalids a sample dose, and when they (naturally) gag at it, the captain orders him to stop.

"'I can't allow it. Men's lives mustn't be sacrificed for an experiment.'"

"'Tain't an experiment,' ses the mate very indignant, 'it's an old family medicine.'

"'Well, they shan't have any more,' ses the captain firmly.

"'Look here,' ses the mate. 'If I kill any one o' these men I'll give you twenty pound. Honour bright, I will.'

"'Make it twenty-five,' ses the skipper, considering." Even the idealists in Jacobs's world have a strong practical streak.

The mate then informs the four invalids that, for his grandmother's remedy to work, they must each take a dose every twenty minutes around the clock, and they can't have anything to take the taste out, because that would weaken the effect.

The first of them begins to recover after only six doses; all are back at work within twenty-four hours. The story is one of the most perfectly paced pieces of comedy I know.

The second story is even better. This one is romantic comedy. The little schooner *Jessica* is anchored in the Thames. Jack, the mate, is idly waiting on deck for Captain Alsen to arrive, so they can leave with the tide for a coastal voyage. Soon a waterman rows out from Tower Quay with not one but two passengers—the captain and his daughter Hetty, a pretty girl of twenty. She is coming along, not at all willingly. "'It's like this, Jack,' the skipper explains to the startled mate. 'There's a friend o' mine, a provision dealer in a large way o' business, wants to marry my girl, and me an' the missus want him to marry her, so, 'o course she wants to marry someone else.'"

The parents' plan is to keep her at sea until she decides to marry the right one. As part of the plan, her father has brought along a large photograph of Mr. Towson, the provision dealer, to keep Hetty reminded of him. (Photographs still had novelty value then.) This he puts up in the cabin.

Jack he assigns the role of praising the photograph and generally encouraging the marriage.

Where to put up Hetty herself is trickier. The "cabin" on a merchant ship is where the officers dine—all two of them on the *Jessica*—and have such indoor life as they do have. She can't sleep there. The total of other accomodations consists of the captain's stateroom, the fo'c'sle, Jack's tiny berth, and a spare berth currently used for storing potatoes and onions. This is where her father decides Hetty should stay, even though the dead cockroach they find as soon as they start taking the onions out has left her extremely reluctant.

"'Why not,'" says the mate, who is enchanted with Hetty, "'why not let her have your stateroom?'

"'Cos I want it myself,' the other replied calmly." Fathers are like that in Jacobs.

Obeying the captain's orders, Jack tries to strike up a friendship with Hetty, though she is distinctly cool. He does discover, however, that she not only has no wish to marry Mr. Towson, she has been seeing her other and younger suitor chiefly to irritate her father. "I can't understand a girl caring for any man," she says airily. "Great clumsy, ugly things."

Jack then gets his bright idea. If she pretends to fall in love with someone on the ship, he points out, her father will be forced to give up his plan and let her go home. Hetty sees the sense in this—she's very tired of living in the former onion bin—and suggests a good-looking sailor named Harry.

Jack quickly answers that that would be bad for ship's discipline. Only an officer would be suitable. Since there are just two, and her father one of them, that naturally narrows the candidates down to him. "Anything to get home again," she says, obliquely accepting his offer.

At this point a three-way strategy begins. Jack's aim is to

turn pretense into reality, while keeping the skipper thinking he's just working for Towson. Hetty's aims are more complex: to frustrate her father's plan, to make the voyage more amusing by setting the mate all sorts of tasks—at one point she dares him to dab mustard on the nose of Towson's portrait—and possibly to see just how serious Jack is. She has, of course, been aware of his interest in her from the beginning.

Then there is the skipper's strategy. Secrets are hard to keep on a ship that small, and when Jack actually does begin to make some progress, Captain Alsen soon finds out. His aim is to break up the new romance without revealing that he knows about it.

Once again the timing is perfect. Hetty is as enchanting to the reader (of either sex) as she is to Jack. And her father is wonderfully funny as a man who regards himself, not entirely mistakenly, as a master of human psychology.

Not all of Jacobs's stories are as good as these two. It would be a miracle if they were. He wrote several hundred stories over the course of a long life—he was born in 1863 and died in 1943—and sometimes he repeats himself or is a bit mechanical. But the best third are wonderful. Never condescending and seldom false, W. W. Jacobs made glorious comedy out of lives that to most people would have seemed brutal or humdrum, or both.

Many Cargoes.
W. W. Jacobs. 1896.

23

Men in Boxcars

One hot afternoon about twenty-five years ago, a teenage boy stood at the edge of a truck stop in central Indiana, thumb out. He was hitching across the country from Boston to California.

Another and much older hitchhiker stood not far away. Rides were few, and the two got to talking. Their highly practical subject: the best way to travel cross-country at little or no cost. The older man proceeded to put the case for freight trains. He had a thousand stories to tell, stories that made hitchhiking by car seem a tame business indeed. (Why was he doing it himself then? Because he was on a brief detour away from any railroad line.)

Before the two parted company, having shared a ride part way across Indiana in a cattle trailer, the older man had identified himself as Chicago Slim, an off-and-on hobo for thirty-five years. He had explained a great deal about railroads and hoboes both. He had shared his mission-donated lunch and his cheap wine.

As for the teenager, that was Michael Mathers, later the author of this book. Inspired by Slim's stories, he hopped his own first freight the very next day. A wild ride into Illinois on a gondola car filled with heaving and shifting pipes both thrilled and terrified him—and when a big pipe slammed into the back wall of the gondola a few inches from his head, very nearly killed him. He went the rest of the way to California less eventfully, doing standard hitchhiking.

But as the terror faded, the thrill revived. He came back home mostly in boxcars (far safer than the open gondolas), and by the time he reached Massachusetts he was hooked. All during college he rode freight trains out west for summer jobs, and rode them home again in the fall. He came to know many hoboes, though as yet he did not spend any nights in their "jungles."

After graduation, he continued to use this inexpensive form of transportation, only now he carried three cameras and a tape recorder with him, and he did stay in jungles. He was consciously preparing to write a book.

Usually books written in this deliberate way suffer for it. Setting out with tape machine and camera and probably an advance from a publisher to capture some colorful bit of life leads to a whole range of problems. At one extreme you wind up depending on your machines to write the book for you. Take a lot of pictures. Record a lot of interviews. Pick the best of each. Then stitch in a little narrative, and voila! a book. Right. A slick, unthinking, commercial book with no point of view.

At the other extreme, there's a point of view all right, but not much landscape to be seen from it. The author is so conscious of himself as doing Something Interesting that he winds up occupying. most of the foreground himself. He's gone, perhaps, to visit the rain forest in Surinam. The book begins with the entire story of how he raised the money for the trip. Soon you get the big incident about the airline surcharge for his cameras, the humorous moment when he ran out of film on the Rio Tapioca, his first encounter with a Guianan bullet tree. What you don't get is Surinam.

You do get hoboes in Michael Mathers's *Riding the Rails*. And railroads. And drama. And stunning pictures. And a sense of having yourself stayed in a jungle, and having yourself crossed the continental divide in an open boxcar. Whatever dangers there are in deliberately having an experience in order to write a book about it, Mathers has avoided them all—in part, perhaps, because love of his subject preceded any thought of exploiting it.

The book has three separate strands, deftly interwoven. First is Mathers's own narrative, beginning at that teenage moment when he met Chicago Slim. He's a born writer, and he knows exactly how present in the narrative to be—just which few of his own adventures belong in a book that centers on hobo life.

Then there are the sixty-five full-page photographs. Somewhere around forty of them are of the kind you might want to cut out and have framed, or form a committee for the sole purpose of awarding prizes to, and the other twenty-five aren't bad either. Mathers had the advantage, to be sure, that his Interesting Material is exceptionally so. Hoboes tend to have character-filled faces and striking clothes. They photograph well. Four pictures in the book include a man called Denver Red. (Having given up families, hoboes generally give up family names too.) Though Red's actual facial structure is quite different from that of our Civil War president, each of the four shots reminds me of a slightly dissolute Abraham Lincoln. There is the same brooding quality, the same homely strength, the same touch of sorrow. Red is not alone. Hoboes like Shorty and Step-and-a-half and Pasco Slim have memorable faces, too. And as for the scenery, a view of a mountain peak above Stevens Pass, Montana, framed by the open doors of a boxcar with three tramps sitting in it . . . it's enough to make an easterner like me think I'd better hurry up and move west to start a new life. I could hop a grain car, maybe.

Finally, there are the seventy or so tape-recorded quotations from hoboes scattered through the book. Here, too, Mathers benefitted from the nature of his material: hoboes also have strong things to say. Some, indeed, are folk philosophers. The same impulse that drove them onto the rails has kept them puzzling about the meaning of life.

But clearly the material also benefitted from Mathers. That is, clearly he drew out these relatively inarticulate men. To some people they would not have talked at all. With some they might have talked, but warily. But Mathers, an ideal listener, brought out the best and deepest in them—and also the funniest and most casual. The man called Black Jesus, for example, will sit down and really think out why he's a hobo, why, as he says, "I always got the yearning and desire to take a journey." Or dark-eyed Sundance will tell what sounds like a traditional tall tale about the fastest and the slowest freights he has ever hopped. It might almost be Paul Bunyan talking.

"I rode so fast on a hotshot one time I passed a mudhole and a tomato patch and they was a mile apart. I passed them so goddam fast they looked like tomato soup. After that I caught a local—a real slow train and he stopped at every house, and when we come to a two-family house we stopped twice. That was in Arkansas."

That's a beautifully paced story. *Riding the Rails* is a beautifully paced book. It is one of the gems of photojournalism—and there are not many.

Riding the Rails.
Michael Mathers. 1973.

24

A Man of Many Letters

Some people have a gift for friendship. A few have a further gift. They not only readily make friends, they bring out the best in anyone they meet, so that to be in their presence is more or less to become one's ideal self.

Sir Sydney Cockerell had this double gift, and he had it in a particularly fortunate time and place. Born a coal merchant's son in Victorian England, he grew up to be something we hardly have a word for in our language—not just a man of letters, but a man of the arts. His great interests as a young man were illuminated manuscripts, architecture, bookbinding (he was William Morris's secretary), and poetry. In 1908, at the age of forty-one, he became director of the Fitzwilliam Museum in Cambridge, and for the next three decades spent much of his time thinking about paintings, sculpture, and prints. His ability gently to extract these objects from rich Englishmen became legendary. He transformed the Fitzwilliam into the distinguished institution it now is.

What was so fortunate about Cockerell's time was that friends still normally communicated by letter. And what was so fortunate about place was that England was still at the height of self-assurance—the present contraction into envy and doubt had not yet occurred. At least in the upper and middle classes, generosity of spirit was routine.

In this golden time and place, Cockerell kept up a steady correspondence with whole bunches of interesting people. Letters poured in. George Bernard Shaw used him as a confidant. So did T. H. White—he was one of the few human be-

ings the author of *The Once and Future King* had much use
for. So did the poet Siegfried Sassoon. So did the young Alec
Guinness, and Freya Stark, and Walter de la Mare. But
poets, novelists, playwrights, and actors were only the beginning. There were people of all sorts. Field Marshal Wavell
wrote him regularly. There was an enclosed Benedictine nun,
Dame Laurentia McLachlan, with whom Cockerell had a
lively correspondence for forty-six years. (Each wrote the
other about 750 letters.) There were relatively obscure people
like William Ivins, for many years Keeper of Prints at the
Metropolitan Museum in New York; like the talented book-
binder Katie Adams; like the minor English politician Lord
Kennet of the Dene.

The Best of Friends contains some hundreds of the letters
these people wrote Sydney Cockerell between 1900 and 1954
and a few of his replies. I can hardly think of a nicer book for
bedtime reading. If "civilization" means anything at all, it
means the kind of environment that fosters communication
like this. There is so much affection, intelligence, humor,
and ripe wisdom in these letters as to make one actually
homesick for the period. There is also the fascination of reading comments by one distinguished person about another,
here on a higher level than in your usual political memoir or
book of namedropping.

To take a complex example, Cockerell delighted in C. M.
Doughty's *Arabia Deserta* (naturally he had known Doughty)
and often pushed his friends to read it. In 1944, he finally got
Shaw started, at an advanced age, and in two successive
letters Shaw gives the book an elaborate stamp of approval.
Somehow T. H. White heard about this, and in *his* next letter
he commented, "How odd of Shaw to wait till he was 88 before reading Doughty. On the whole I would not call him an
educated man, for his age."

The thread that holds the book together is Sydney Cockerell himself. Though you see so few of his own letters, reflections of him constantly appear in the letters to him. There he is in the middle, the perfect listener and appreciator, to whom Freya Stark brilliantly describes the conference that led to the independence of India, and Alex Guinness—movingly— the effect of a toy wooden duck on the children of a war-ravaged Greek village in 1944. He sends presents, usually books. He introduces one friend to another—the playwright to the nun, for example. The nun being enclosed, the playwright has to go to Stanbrook Abbey and talk through a double grille. Soon the two are calling each other Brother Bernard and Sister Laurentia and having a correspondence of their own.

But there are other threads as well. Nearly every letter touches one way or another on books, either as literature or as esthetic objects in their own right. A surprising number of the friends share Cockerell's own interest in the physical act of writing—that is, they are calligraphers or at least lovers of calligraphy. Lord Kennet of the Dene, having lost his right arm in the First World War, learns to write a beautiful half-uncial script with his left. Siegfried Sassoon, looking at a Latin book once owned and signed by Thomas Hardy (Cockerell has just sent it to him), writes, "That signature of his is like order in chaos, isn't it? (& craftsmanship in a world of machines!) " Dame Laurentia, an expert and a medievalist, says casually, "I cannot warm up to any writing later than the 12th century, except the Italian 15th century." Ivins, the American, devotes a whole letter to comparing "real" hand-writing to the showpieces of the professionals. He has some samples of writing by people like the Sforzas, dukes of Milan, in the sixteenth century. "How much more wonderful they were," he says, "than the writing-books. Written, so to say, with the voices of authority, and with any pen whatever, new-sharpened or worn to a stump, but the swing all there, adapting itself as something alive to the quill that chance brought under the hand. Can it be that the decay (or whatever) of handwriting can be traced to the incoming of metal nibs that don't wear rapidly and idiosyncratically in use? . . . I'm sure that fellows such as the mature Titians and Rembrandts painted with almost any brushes they picked up, just as they drew with anything that would make a mark. For them it was the will of the gesture that counted, not its mechanical perfection."

In *The Best of Friends*, we are in a very different world than that of the word processor—a slower world and perhaps a more human one.

In the end, it's the humanity of it that makes the book so delightful. Sydney Cockerell gave his friends both attention and love, and they returned it with interest. Such loving attention to the courtesies and nuances of friendship. Such receptivity to other minds. Such delight in art and nature both. One would wish these part of any life.

Bernard Berenson, meaning to describe only himself, gives the flavor of the whole book in a letter he wrote Cockerell in 1946. Berenson was eighty-one, living in the poverty of postwar Italy, Cockerell seventy-nine, surrounded by the austerity of postwar England. "I am ageing," Berenson wrote, "getting feebler, more jumpy, too curious about events of all kinds, see too many people, undertake too much, but between aches pains & exhaustion enjoy life ecstatically. How can one avoid it, living in this beautiful world?"

> *The Best of Friends:*
> *Further Letters to Sydney*
> *Carlyle Cockerell.*
> Ed. Viola Meynell. 1956.

25

Love, Longing, and Death

Novelists seldom blossom early. Poets do it all the time, but the number of young writers who write really good fiction is quite modest. The number who with their first novel achieve full mastery is tiny. Mailer managed it with *The Naked and the Dead* at twenty-five, and Fitzgerald with *This Side of Paradise* at twenty-four. Stephen Crane beat them both with *The Red Badge of Courage* at twenty-three—in fact he strode in at twenty-two, if you want to count his privately published *Maggie*. (I don't.) The usual case is a Melville, or Bellow, or Faulkner, or Henry James reaching the top of his form only after a thorough apprenticeship.

Peter Beagle is one of the glorious exceptions. His senior year in college he wrote a novel about love, longing, and death. The next year Viking published it. The year was 1960, and Beagle was twenty-one years old. Whoever at Viking wrote the jacket blurb composed the usual fatuities and then concluded, "It would not be at all surprising if this novel became a minor classic." The blurb-writer was correct. *A Fine and Private Place* is an astonishingly good book: a pure and perfect comedy with tragic overtones.

The book opens in a large cemetery in the borough of the Bronx, New York City. The first two characters you meet are a man who has been living as as recluse in the cemetery for nineteen years, and a raven who has been supplying him with food for all that time. Both are quintessential New York Jews. Jonathan Rebeck, the man, is gentle, philosophic, scholarly—a former pharmacist for whom the weight of life simply became too much. Now he keeps house in an old mausoleum in Yorkchester Cemetery and plays a little chess. The raven, clearly a descendent of those who fed the prophet Elijah, is tough, urban, and funny. He also talks.

On page one, the raven arrives with an unusually large contribution to Mr. Rebeck's larder: a whole baloney he has picked up at a delicatessen. It's a heavy load, the raven is out of breath, and Mr. Rebeck feels guilty. You don't have to keep doing this, he says apologetically. The raven explodes.

"'Once a year,' he said hoarsely. 'Once a year you get worried. You start wondering how come the airborne Gristede's. You say to yourself, What's he getting out of it?'" And goes on to remind Rebeck that it's the doom of ravens—"we're pretty neurotic birds"—to look after troubled beings. When Mr. Rebeck reaches out to stroke him, he winces. "Don't do that," he says. "It makes me nervous."

Soon the raven is off to other business, flying out several empty paper bags as he goes. (He is infinitely more practical than Mr. Rebeck about keeping the mausoleum looking unlived-in.) At the same time, a small funeral procession enters Yorkchester, heading for the Catholic section. They're burying Michael Morgan, a brilliant thirty-four-year-old history professor, to whose point of view the book now shifts. He is in his coffin, quite conscious and quite dead.

He and the reader simultaneously learn what death means. In Peter Beagle's world, there is neither immortality nor extinction. Instead, there's a sort of limited continuation as a sort of ghost. You are ghostly in that you no longer eat, drink, sleep, or get tired. Nor can you touch anything or anybody. To most living people you are invisible and inaudible, though the other dead see and hear you well enough.

How long this state lasts depends on how much you loved life. If you were only mildly fond of it, you begin to forget who you were within a week or two, dimming out like a stage light. If you were passionately alive, you may keep consciousness for several years. Meanwhile, you are confined to the place of the dead—that is, to the cemetery in which your body is buried.

Michael Morgan is one of the passionate. His ghost is out of the coffin within minutes and beginning to explore the cemetery. By evening he is playing chess with Mr. Rebeck, one of the two living people in the book who can see him. Rebeck, of course, has to make his moves for him, since he can't touch the chess pieces. Morgan is also explaining furiously that his beautiful wife Sandra poisoned him.

Here are our two main male characters. The two main women soon appear. The first is Gertrude Klapper, a widow. Her husband, the late Morris Klapper, is ensconced in a mausoleum not far from the one in which Mr. Rebeck lives, and she comes fairly often to visit it. She's a nice-looking woman in her forties, no intellectual, but full of common sense and a kind of urban gallantry. The other is Laura Durand, who's dead. A truck hit her. Alive, she was a rather plain, clumsy, very bright woman of twenty-nine who worked in a bookstore.

Two love affairs ensue. Mrs. Klapper encounters Jonathan Rebeck, the recluse, and gradually wins him back to life outside the cemetery. And the ghost of Michael Morgan falls in love with the ghost of Laura Durand.

The two affairs are very different in their flavor. Gertrude Klapper, though she's not a virtuoso wit like the raven, is full of wry Yiddish humor—she also has a sentimental streak a yard wide—and her redemption of the shy pharmacist has a comic side. But Laura Durand and Michael Morgan are both flaming romantics. Add that at best they have a very short time, and that they can love with words only, and you have a situation of rare intensity. There is a scene worthy of Cyrano de Bergerac when they attempt—and, of course, fail—to hold hands. There is another where they sit invisibly on the cemetery wall at dawn, watching, loving, and envying a Bronx boy and his girl who have been up all night and who between kisses are deciding that they will go together to explain their (innocent) escapade to the girl's parents. A reader who's not moved by that scene is (a) blind to good writing, and (b) stonyhearted. In fact, that's true for the whole novel. You don't even have to accept the possibility of ghosts to be moved, because of course what Peter Beagle is really talking about is the temporariness of everything and the apartness that is present in even the closest human touching.

After long thought, I have been able to find just two flaws in the book. (Not counting, that is, Beagle's shameful failure to write about every person, living or dead, in the whole Bronx, instead of a mere twenty or so.) One is that Mrs. Klapper's role as bearer of the life-force doesn't quite fit with her sharply drawn individual personality as a lonely and somewhat ineffectual widow trying to get through the long days since Morris died. The other is that Beagle, at least at twenty-one, was not a particularly good observer of nature. One of the funniest scenes in the whole book is an encounter between the raven—en route to Rebeck with a roast beef sandwich, and at this point hopping a ride in the back of a cemetery truck—and a poetic red squirrel. The squirrel's lines alone would mark Beagle as a great comic writer. But anyone who's even moderately familiar with squirreline behavior would know that red squirrels don't have so much as a glimmer of poetry in their souls. That should have been a gray squirrel.

A Fine and Private Place.
Peter S. Beagle. 1960.

26

Philip Larkin's Greatest Poem

Which are the great poems of the twentieth century? In English, that is. Some of Frost's, certainly. Some of T. S. Eliot's. Several by Yeats, several by Auden. One also by the English poet Philip Larkin.

Larkin is hardly an unknown poet. His is one of the names that have general though minor currency. Like William Carlos Williams, or Richard Wilbur, or Marianne Moore, he holds a sure place in the anthologies, and in the reference books, too.

But there is no line of his you can count on people to recognize—no world ending with a whimper, no rough beast slouching along, no fences making good neighbors. There is no book of his everybody has read. Surprisingly few people realize that Larkin has written one of the great poems of our time.

That poem is called "Church Going." Fundamentalists of all sects should probably avoid it, because its sensibility is so alien to their own. Most other people will find it profoundly moving. That's especially true for people who don't even believe in profundity (or in being moved). They will be hit hardest of all.

The poem is written in the anti-heroic style that is Larkin's specialty, and also the hallmark of our time. Fervor and lofty emotion are conspicuously lacking. As the poem begins,

Larkin is on a bicycle tour and has stopped in some little English village to look at the parish church. His pause has nothing to do with piety, still less with wanting a chance to say a prayer. He's popping in tourist-style to check out the architecture.

> Once I am sure there's nothing going on
> I step inside, letting the door thud shut.
> Another church: matting, seats, and stone,
> And little books; sprawlings of flowers, cut
> For Sunday, brownish now; some brass and stuff
> Up at the holy end; the small neat organ;
> And a tense, musty unignorable silence,
> Brewed God knows how long.

The first line gives a strong clue to how the poem works. On the surface, it merely says the poet, like any prudent tourist, makes sure there's no service occurring in this nameless church before he strolls in. But underneath, "nothing going on" has another implication: that the church no longer has any significance.

Once inside, he looks around with a secular, almost a derisive eye. "Little books," as if he didn't know they were Church of England prayer books and hymnals. "Brass and stuff"—he is emotionally distant from the very concept of sacred objects. "The holy end" is downright mocking.

But already a counterpoint has begun. That silence may be musty, but there is a power in it. Enough to change the poet's mood? It's hard to tell.

> Hatless, I take off
> My cycle-clips in awkward reverence,
> Move forward, run my hand around the font.

Here is what could be taken as a genuflection but is really just a bicyclist bending down to remove the ankle clips that keep his trousers from getting caught in the chain. And then we get our answer. The poet begins to make free with the empty church. The silence does *not* awe him—not yet, anyway. In fact, he casually dispels it.

> Mounting the lectern, I peruse a few
> Hectoring large-scale verses, and pronounce
> 'Here endeth' much more loudly than I'd meant.
> The echoes snigger briefly. Back at the door
> I sign the book, donate an Irish sixpence,
> Reflect the place was not worth stopping for.

Again there's a double meaning. On the surface, the poet is just imitating an Episcopal minister. Twice during the service of morning prayer, the minister goes to the lectern and reads a lesson from the Bible, one each from the Old Testament and the New. When he's done, he says, "Here endeth the lesson"—or at least he did until recently, when the Episcopal Church underwent its own little *aggiornamento*. Underneath, of course, the passage suggests that here endeth Christianity.

The rest of the poem is a meditation on that ending. The poet begins to wonder what will happen to little churches like this as faith dies out. Will they be abandoned, as the great abbeys were in Henry VIII's time? Will a few be kept as museums, and the rest degenerate into places of superstition? Yes, he thinks, they will. Old crones will come to touch a particular stone, and children will fear ghosts among the old graves outside.

Even that won't last, however.

> But superstition, like belief, must die,
> And what remains when disbelief has gone?
> Grass, weedy pavement, brambles, buttress, sky.

This is the low point of the poem. The church has been drained of all value whatsoever; there is nothing left but a heap of meaningless stone, over which the briars grow. And then with seeming casualness Larkin starts to reintroduce meaning. He idly wonders who will be the very last visitor to stand where he is standing now, knowing that here was a church. He imagines several possibilities. It might be a "ruin-bibber, randy for antique." It might be a scholar, taking notes on the old building for an article. If the last visit occurs sooner than that, before services have completely ceased, it might be the sort of Christian-by-habit of which the Church of England is currently full, as American churches are, too. That is, someone who comes once or twice a year, usually with his or her family, for one of the great festival services. In that case, it would be what Larkin calls a "Christmas-addict, counting on a whiff / Of gown-and-bands and organ-pipes and myrrh."

And then there is a fourth possibility. The last visitor might be someone like Larkin himself. Here the poem soars. It becomes so splendid that the only sensible thing is to quote the whole two-stanzas-and-a-line with which it ends.

> Or will he be my representative,
>
> Bored, uninformed, knowing the ghostly silt
> Dispersed, yet tending to this cross of ground
> Through suburb scrub because it held unspilt
> So long and equably what since is found
> Only in separation—marriage, and birth,
> And death, and thoughts of these—for which was built
> This special shell? For, though I've no idea
> What this accoutered frowsty barn is worth,
> It pleases me to stand in silence here;
>
> A serious house on serious earth it is,
> In whose blent air all our compulsions meet,
> Are recognized, and robed as destinies.
> And that much never can be obsolete,

Since someone will forever be surprising
A hunger in himself to be more serious,
And gravitating with it to this ground,
Which, he once heard, was proper to grow wise in,
If only that so many dead lie round.

Here, I think, are the best lines Philip Larkin has ever written, and among the best done in this century. Here is an elegy written in a country church, and it is profounder than the one Gray wrote outside in the churchyard. The elegy is for Christianity itself, that great force, which could take ordinary human drives and robe them as destinies. The irreverent tourist has recognized the power of the brooding silence, and he has given it such an accolade as no mere believer possibly could.

"Church Going."
Philip Larkin. 1955.

27

Quest of the Mulla-Mulgars

In the Forest of Munza-mulgar live three brothers, monkeys of high descent. Thumma and Thimbulla, the two older brothers, are strong and intelligent (as monkeys go). Ummanodda, known as Nod, the youngest brother, is smaller and much more given to rash action than his siblings. But he also has the little velvety patch on his head that shows him to be a *nizza-neela*, or as one would say in human speech, a being able to work magic.

The mother of these three is an ordinary gray fruit-monkey, accustomed to scrambling about on all fours. But their father—their father is a *mulla-mulgar*, a royal monkey. He had come to the forest late in life, worn and racked by years of wandering. But he had come walking upright, as men walk, wearing a red jacket, carrying the Wonderstone, and followed by his servant. Long ago he had set out from the court of his brother, the Prince of the Valleys of Tishnar, to see the world.

The young fruit-monkey nursed this proud old wanderer back to health, and for thirteen years Seelem stayed with her. The three sons that were born to them he taught things that very few monkeys know: how to make fire, how to count, how to take honey from bees without being stung. "But, above all, he taught them to walk upright, never to taste blood, and never, unless in danger or despair, to climb trees."

In the fourteenth year, a longing came on the old prince to see again the Valleys of Tishnar. He promised to return if successful and take his family there. But no word ever came. Seasons passed; the mother sickened and died. That same year, snow fell in the forest for the first time in memory, and after Nod accidentally burnt the hut in which they were living, the sons decide to set out on their father's track.

So begins Walter de la Mare's *The Three Royal Monkeys*. It is a children's book like very few others in our language. In some ways it's a classic quest story, carefully following the traditions of the youngest-son-as-hero and the test by ordeal. But it is both wilder and stranger than most quest stories, and it is far richer in language. It is thus not a book for every child but only for those with active imaginations and perhaps some taste for unfamiliar words.

There are two strange things about the book. One, of course, is the simian setting. The characters are both more and less like human beings than is usual in a good children's book about animals. In the usual case—even, say, in so stunning a book as Richard Adams's *Watership Down*—the animals behave like their own species, but their emotions are those of human beings. Rabbit actions, human feelings in the case of *Watership Down*. The lines are more blurred in de la Mare. One might expect them to be. Monkeys and apes are the closest to us, anyway; there were monkeys in red jackets long before old Seelem. Monkeys can love and hate and envy as no rabbit or mole ever did.

But I mean more than that. I mean that de la Mare has given the three young *mulla-mulgars* emotions and thoughts that are human enough to be recognizable but animal enough to be alien and even uncanny.

The other strangeness comes from the setting. It is a long

journey indeed from the forest to the Valleys of Tishnar, and de la Mare has richly imagined every inch of it. The three brothers encounter many other monkey cultures. For a time they are prisoners of the *minimuls*, flesh-eating monkeys who live underground. They are helped, in one of the most splendid parts of the book, by a rather forlorn tribe of mountain monkeys—mountaineers who use their own bodies as climbing equipment. (They get up and down cliffs by forming ladders, each lower monkey holding by the hands to the feet of the monkey above, the lightest monkey at the bottom. About twenty is their limit, and roughly that many of themselves they call a "rope.")

Nod even encounters a man, a shipwrecked sailor named Andy Battle, with whom he lives for a time, half as pet and half as companion. There are fierce baboons, and river-monkeys who fish with their tails. All of these, except Andy Battle, are like the royal brothers themselves—something more than animal and something less than human. They are not parodies of us, and not even quite distortions, but eerie reflections. And one of the eeriest aspects is the utter absence of morality. Of course these monkeys judge particular things to be good or bad. It is good to have plenty of *ukka*-nuts and bad to be eaten by the *minimuls*. It is good to be able to make a fire in the snow, bad to lose the Wonderstone (as Nod twice does). But there is no Law of the Jungle, such as Kipling imagined, no eternal struggle between good and evil, as in *The Lord of the Rings*. Things just happen, sometimes with rhyme, never with reason. Perhaps that is a little like childhood itself.

I've saved the best for last. De la Mare had a happy ear for language. Without being systematic about it—there are no neat appendices, as in so much science fiction and heroic fantasy—he has invented a really fine monkey language. Some of it is quite independent of human speech. The word for "monkey" itself is *mulgar*. A *munza-mulgar* is a forest-monkey, and a *mulla-mulgar* is, of course, a royal one. A man—the word recognizes our kinship—is an *oomgar*. *Meermut* is a literal shadow, or a ghost, "or even the pictured remembrance of anything in the mind."

Some of it, on the other hand, is human speech made strange. Once, in great danger, with the aid of the Wonder-stone, Nod summons three of the Little Horses of Tishnar, and he and his brothers escape astride them. Later one learns that these little horses are also called *zevveras*, and that they are striped black and white. It is then not too hard to figure out what an *oomgar* would call them.

One can even see this part of the language in the process of creation, as when Nod later refers to the shipwrecked sailor as his *messimut*, and one realizes that this is how he has heard Andy Battle's word "messmate," or nautical dinner companion. Mulgar is a beautiful, poetic, though occasionally scary language, and worth the encountering.

I don't want to make too high a claim for the book. It will not prepare children for life in the computer age, or teach them tolerance, or make them wise. But those who are imaginative it will surely give pleasure to. And one might even fancy that if all us *oomgar* learned to walk upright, never to taste blood, and never, except in danger or despair, to climb trees, our species might yet make its way out of the blizzard of modern history and into the sunlit Valleys of Tishnar.

The Three Royal Monkeys.
Walter de la Mare. 1910.

28

Prisoner in Wartime Italy

It has been estimated that something like forty million people were prisoners at one time or another during World War II. Several million of them made one or more attempts to escape, and some hundreds of thousands of them succeeded. French civilians escaped from Japanese internment camps in Vietnam; German military prisoners escaped from camps in the United States (by the end of the war we had five hundred POW camps scattered across the country, from which about a hundred Germans escaped each month); American fliers climbed over the walls of castles in Saxony. Most of the escapees—a lot of them, anyway—later wrote books about their adventures. The World War II Prisoner Escape Book is a large and recognized genre, like the Vietnam Grunt Book or the My Thirty Years in Diplomacy Book.

Eric Newby's *When the Snow Comes, They Will Take You Away* is simultaneously one of the best and one of the most unusual escape books yet written. What makes it good is the writing. What makes it unusual is that the author is not the hero of his own escape—though he is obviously a brave man. Instead there is a heroine: the daring and strong-willed girl who engineered the escape for him. And there is a whole group of lesser heroes: Italian farmers who at fearful risk contrive to hide this enemy stranger, an Italian doctor who saves him under the very noses of the Germans simply because helping Allied POWs is the one thing he can do at that moment to express his antifascism, and so on.

In the summer of 1942, Eric Newby was one of six British soldiers who paddled in to a Sicilian beach from a waiting submarine. There was a big German airfield on the island, from which bombers regularly flew out and sank most of the Allied ships heading for Malta. Lacking any better means of counterattack, the British dispatched this six-man army. Its orders: penetrate the beach defenses, cut through the wire surrounding the airfield, get onto the runways, and then blow up as many bombers as possible. They almost succeeded— and then they were captured.

The next year Newby spent in an Italian POW camp. He and several hundred other British officers were shipped to a former orphanage in the little town of Fontanellato, near Parma. Most were men in their early twenties. Newby himself was twenty-two.

Aside from digging escape tunnels, their chief diversion was looking at the girls of Fontanellato. This was a daily if somewhat risky pleasure. There were almost no young men left in the town, and the local girls had as *their* chief diversion an evening stroll down the road in front of the orphanage. To watch was forbidden; the guards had standing orders to shoot at any face seen in a window. Naturally the young Englishmen stared anyway, and usually in perfect safety for the first minute or two. As Newby puts it, "The effect of these visions [the girls] on the wretched Italian guards who were immured high up in their watchtowers, was as powerful as it was on us. Utterly distracted, they turned their backs on the *orfanotrofio* in order to look at them more closely, until some N.C.O., old enough and sour enough to be indifferent to women, screeched at them so loudly that they whirled around and, seeing us, discharged their rifles. And he adds, "But not even the Italian Army in its most bellicose mood was able to stop us looking at the girls of Fontanellato, or the girls at us."

On September 9, 1943, in the middle of the huge turmoil caused by Mussolini's surrender and the German takeover in Italy, the whole group of officers escaped. Many were soon recaptured, however, including Newby, who was at something of a disadvantage for cross-country flight because he had a broken ankle. While still free, though, he met and was helped by one of the girls of Fontanellato, a slender blonde who spoke English with a strong middle-European accent. "Wonce I have seen you in the *orfanotrofio* and you vaved and the *soldati* went pom pom," she says. Then she tells him to start learning Italian, because he is going to need it to survive as an escapee. He persuades her to become his teacher, and he promptly falls in love.

This girl, though an Italian citizen, is Slovene by birth, from territory ceded to Italy after World War I. Her father, deported from the new territory lest he foment Slovenian national sentiment, teaches school in Fontanellato. Her name is Wanda.

Wanda, her father, and the local doctor soon get Newby free again, and the doctor takes him—driving boldly right through a convoy of the 16th Panzer Division—to the mountains where he is to hide.

All that is a mere prelude to the main part of the book, which is the story of Newby's life in hiding. During most of the fall he lived and worked on a remote mountain farm, on the Plan del Sotto. Luigi, the farmer, is well aware that the German commander in Parma will put to death anyone caught sheltering a POW, and chooses to take the young Englishman in anyway. He also strikes a hard bargain. Mountain farms in the Apennines are as stony and barren as mountain farms in New England. Newby's task all fall is to pick stones out of Luigi's fields, load them in a handcart, push the cart to the edge of a cliff, and dump them over. He does this in exchange for board and room. Meanwhile, he is ceasing to be Lieutenant Newby, and (Eric being unpronounceable in Italian) is becoming Enrico the farmhand.

The account of life on the Pian del Sotto is one of those stories that, if you read it, will stick in your mind forever. There is the hard-working and rather eccentric life of the farm itself. Enrico missed not one detail of Italian peasant life, which he has the Englishman's capacity to admire and find funny simultaneously. There are his adventures on Sundays, the day he doesn't have to pick rock. One Sunday, for example, he climbs a mountain, just to be alone for the day, and in the afternoon he takes a nap. When he wakes up, a young German officer is standing over him.

Enrico claims, of course, to be Italian; the German is not convinced. "'I think that you are English,' he said finally, in English. 'English, or from one of your colonies. You cannot be an English deserter; you are on the wrong side of the battle front. You do not look like a parachutist or a saboteur. You must be a prisoner of war. That is so, is it not?'"

The German goes on to make clear that he has no intention of making a capture. Instead he offers Newby a bottle of beer, and the two young men sit down to discuss life. Oberleutnant Frick used to teach botany at Gottingen; now he is assigned to give lectures on Renaissance art at a German R & R center. ("'To soldiers,'" he says sadly, "'who are engaged in destroying these things as hard as they are able. Do you not think it strange?'" Newby doesn't, pointing out that the British and American armies do exactly the same.)

This conversation gets more and more moving, as one finds that Frick has no illusions whatsoever about his country's role. "'It is not pleasant to be disliked,'" he tells Newby, "'and it is very unpleasant to be a German and to know that one is hated because one *is* German and, because, collectively, we are wrong in what we are doing. That is why I hate this war, or one of the reasons. And of course, because of this, we shall lose it. We must. We have to.'"

It's hardly your typical World War II Prisoner Escape Book conversation. It is merely authentic, in its context utterly heartrending—and, I fear, uncomfortably close to what a citizen of any great power would have to say about the role of his own government right now. It's what a thoughtful Chinese lieutenant might say about Tibet, or a Russian officer about Afghanistan, or an American one about Nicaragua.

There are other and happier adventures, too. There is the dance that Newby goes to at a neighboring farm. There is the adventure in the hayloft with Dolores, the auburn-haired farmgirl on the Pian del Sotto. (Don't worry. Enrico remains true, though just barely, to his Wanda.) And at rare glorious intervals, there are messages that Wanda contrives to get to him. Lest they be intercepted, she normally writes him as Signora Enrica, and enchanting notes she composes. Twice there are actual visits from this enterprising girl, each involving a good deal more risk than Romeo ever took, going over to the Capulets to see Juliet.

There is far more in the book, indeed, than one can possibly summarize, including Enrico's second recapture on December 29, 1943, and including an epilogue about a postwar visit to Italy with Wanda, now his wife. The main purpose of that visit was to see and thank as many as possible of the farmers who had shielded him. (Several couldn't be thanked. They were dead, thanks to the folly of one of the British officers from the orphanage. When this fellow escaped, he took his diary with him and continued to make entries. When the Germans recaptured him, they found it in his pocket, complete with the real names of everybody who had fed or sheltered him.)

If I were rich, I would probably buy about five hundred copies of *When the Snow Comes, They Will Take You Away*. I'd give one to every friend I have who's a reader, and the rest I would send with flattering inscriptions to persons in high places. It's such a charming, funny, lively book they might actually read it. And it's so humanizing that if they did read it, they might find it a little harder to keep making preparations for yet another war.

When the Snow Comes, They Will Take You Away.
Eric Newby. 1971.

29

Ugly Ducklings and Unhappy Swans

Mary Agnes Keeley, thirty-five years old, five feet eleven inches tall, thin as a pencil, lives with her widowed mother in Bridgeport, Connecticut. Her father, a Bridgeport fireman, died when she was fifteen. Right after high school she went to work to help put her brother through college. He is now an FBI agent, assigned to the Buffalo office, with a wife and three children. Mary Agnes is secretary to the president of Standard Zipper in Bridgeport. She is a virgin. She is also in the early stages of martyrdom to her mother, a natural genius at using guilt feelings and ill health to control her children.

That martyrdom does not occur; instead this novel does. Mary Agnes takes the Bridgeport bus. That is, she quits her job, leaves home, and goes to New York. Mary Agnes—only let's call her Ag, as most people do—has always been bright. Her one defiance of her mother over the years has been the taking of a whole series of night courses in literature. She reads voraciously, has ambitions to write.

In fairly short order she *is* writing: advertising copy for a manufacturer of velcro fasteners. She's living in an apartment on Ninth Street, meeting artists, putting on weight. By chapter 5 she has both lost her virginity and begun to write fiction.

This basic plot is a familiar one, because it expresses one of the very commonest of human fantasies. Ugly duckling becomes a swan. Man or woman trapped in boring routine breaks loose, makes a new start, achieves a glamorous life. Seemingly ordinary person proves exceptional. All of us *are* exceptional, at least to ourselves, only the world fails to treat us so. It is deeply gratifying to read about someone who gets a grip on himself or herself and makes the world respond properly.

Maureen Howard's treatment of the theme is something else. In the usual book of this kind—and I am talking about true novels, not easy romances—the Ag character has center stage all to herself, while we, entranced, watch her transformation. And in the usual book of this kind, swanhood turns out to be a really nice thing. Some of the other swans may prove vicious; some of the glitter of the great world may prove to be tinsel; the transformed life may even end in tragedy. But that it is a glorious thing to become a swan, and that the great world is truly great, these assumptions are not questioned.

Bridgeport Bus is not like that. It has three heroines. Ag is certainly the main one—and most of the time the narrator— but there are two other young women whose stories are told and whose presence makes the value of swanhood much more dubious.

One is Lydia Savaard. Ag meets her when she first arrives in New York, and stays briefly at a hotel for women, a genteel place on Fifth Avenue. Lydia is twenty-five, rather mousy, as Protestant as Ag is Catholic. She grew up in a nice, upper-middle-class family, went to Vassar, and then married a young aristocrat just out of Princeton. The Savaards, though they have now lost most of their money, have been high society for two centuries. What Lydia didn't realize, marrying Henry Savaard, was that his upper-classness is a burden he can't handle. He simply can't live up to his concept of what a Savaard should be. He married Lydia principally because he thought Miss Mouse wouldn't see through him, and would join him in worship of the Savaard past. But he sees through himself, and the knowledge breaks him. At twenty-six he is in a mental institution, which is why Lydia is at the women's hotel. She's trying with the aid of pills to sleep twenty hours a day, and in the other four making feeble attempts to get an annulment. (Her lawyer is one of the many superbly drawn minor characters.) Ag partially rouses her from this lethargy, and the two of them take the little apartment on Ninth Street together. It is hard to envy the aristocratic WASP life once you've got to know Lydia and Henry.

The third heroine is Ag's first cousin, Sherry Henderson. Sherry, born Mary Elizabeth Hurley, grew up in Bridgeport even more drably than Ag herself. But she was red-headed, very pretty, irresistibly attractive to men. She took the Bridgeport bus long before Ag. She left at sixteen, became a chorus girl, then a budding starlet. Alas, she didn't have quite enough talent or quite enough sense. Though she stays in the world of luxury and privilege—she eventually marries a wealthy publisher, much older—she is as unable as Henry Savaard to sustain the role of swan. Sherry is a suicide at thirty-three.

And Ag herself? Ag is a survivor. At the end of the book Ag is about to have a baby. Ag has become a very good writer. One of the marvelous things in *Bridgeport Bus* is the interpolated play that occupies about a quarter of the book. Ag wrote it. She herself is one of the characters; the other seven are her parents, her brother, the two Savaards, Sherry, and Stanley Sarnicki, her principal lover in New York. The play is tragic, symbolic, surrealistic—and wildly funny. It is a tremendous tour de force. If only it could stand alone (it can't), I would love to see it on Broadway.

But Ag, tough, perceptive and witty as she is, suffers from

the same malady that Sherry and Lydia and Henry do. It is a malady I know well myself. It is the incapacity to forgive life for being so mundane. My first fully conscious experience of it occurred when I was a young man, in love with a slightly older woman, a divorcee with a small daughter. The three of us were in a supermarket on a Friday night, buying food for the weekend.

The store was packed with other shoppers, mostly harassed. Martha, the little daughter, was crying. Lois, the mother, kept thinking of more grubby things we needed: paper towels, detergent, Wesson oil. In the end it all seemed so unutterably beneath what I wanted life to be like that I began drifting further and further back from the shopping cart (a squalid enough object itself). I didn't want to be associated. Lois, a clever woman, divined at once what was in my mind, and we later had a sharp scene about it.

Ag—and, of course, Maureen Howard behind her—sees almost everywhere that failure of life to be what it should be. If you escape the shopping carts, as on the Savaard estate on Long Island, then you merely have a high-class setting in which the actors mostly fail to sustain their parts. It is the special brilliance of *Bridgeport Bus* that it turns this rueful awareness into gallant and high comedy.

Bridgeport Bus.
Maureen Howard. 1965.

30

In Medieval Japan

About 660 years ago, a distinguished Japanese poet named Urabe no Kaneyoshi resigned his post at the court of the emperor and took vows as a Buddhist priest. He was still a young man, under forty. He didn't leave Kyoto, or enter a monastery, or anything radical like that. He just moved into a cottage some distance away from the palace, though still near enough so that he could see his fashionable friends and hear all the news. He also began to write in prose under his new priestly name of Kenko. (Fourteenth-century Japanese loved changing their names, and often did—but Kenko had special reason. New priestly names are a feature of practically all religions. Pope John, after all, started as Angelo Roncalli. Ramakrishna, until he took Hindu orders, was known was Gadadhar Chatterjee.)

Kenko's principal prose work is a collection of 243 tiny essays, ranging in length from a single sentence to three or four pages. They are in the form the Japanese call *zuihitsu*, meaning scattered thoughts, and they remain to this day the most famous example of *zuihitsu* in all Japanese literture. Many of them also remain as deliciously readable in the 1980s as they were in the 1330s—and not because of their quaint medieval charm, either. On the contrary, one thing that's striking about Kenko is that his sensibility seems so in tune with the contemporary world. He would be quite at home in present-day Japan or America.

Take his views on love, sex, and marriage. Kenko is both romantic and disillusioned, like most of us in 1988. Romantically, he believes that life without love and sex, and preferably the two together, would be barely worth living. Disillusionedly, he knows that getting the two together is hard. "A man may excel at everything else," he begins the third essay, "but if he has no taste for lovemaking, one feels something terribly inadequate about him, as if he were a valuable winecup without a bottom." He goes on to describe the typical lover, "frantically resorting to one unsuccessful stratagem after another; and for all that, most often sleeping alone, though never soundly." Then comes the one alien touch. He has a different notion than ours about who is normally pursuing whom. It is better for a man, he concludes the essay, that "women not consider him an easy conquest."

What about marriage? We tend to think that only in the last couple of centuries has it become a source of spiritual intimacy; before that it was an economic unit, or some crude biological arrangement, or whatever. We are wrong. Kenko considers (essay 240) the case of the young woman who, just because he's rich, marries a vulgar provincial, or some "old priest twice her age." Then he wonders in honest bafflement, "What can they possibly find to talk about?"

Children? Isn't that what the crude biological arrangement was all about? Weren't women in the fourteenth century expected to put in just about full time being pregnant? Not in Kyoto, or at least not in Kenko's circles.

"Even members of the nobility, let alone persons of no consequence, would do well not to have children," he writes in essay 6. "Prince Kaneakira, Fujiwara no Koremichi, and Minamoto no Arihito all desired that their line end with themselves." And he quotes another princely Fujiwara as saying,

"You would best not have descendants. How unfortunate it would be if they proved inferior to yourself!"

Does this mean that Kenko was decadent, a snob, incapable of warm, natural human feelings? It does not. He was certainly a snob, like every other courtier in Kyoto (or Paris, Naples, London), but he had plenty of warm, natural feelings, and they included a full awareness of the joys of parenthood. In essay 142, he quotes a conversation he once overheard between two brutal-looking soldiers.

"Have you got any kids?" asks the first.

"Not one," says the second.

"Then," says the first, "I don't suppose you know what deep feelings are. You probably haven't a drop of human warmth in you. That's a frightening thought. It's having children that makes people understand the beauty of life."

I suspect that Kenko's answer, if one charged him with inconsistency here, would be twofold. I think he'd first say that we all have many moods, and that in some of them parenthood seems like the central experience of life, and in others it seems like twenty years of voluntary servitude. And then I think he'd add that for simple minds like the soldier's, parenthood may indeed be the only way one comes to deep feelings, but that highly civilized courtiers know a dozen other paths.

Kenko feels modern in other ways than his views of love and marriage. He does in his genial scepticism, so at odds with most medieval thinking. Priest though he was, and good Buddhist, he had an almost total lack of superstition. The notion of lucky days, so dear to the oriental heart, merely amused him. He doubts miracles, too. I especially like a little ghost story he tells. In Japanese mythology, demons often assumed the shape of foxes. His story is about one that was haunting the Gojo Palace. "Once when the courtiers were playing *go* in the Black Chamber, someone lifted the blinds and peeped in. 'Who is it?' they cried and turned to look at it. A fox was squatting there, just like a man, watching them. At the shout of 'It's a fox!' the creature became rattled and ran away. It must have been an inexperienced fox, a failure at working spells."

Poor demon, no more luck than the lovers.

Kenko records news and gossip, too. Some of it has lost its interest after six hundred years, especially when it turns on details of court ritual. But some remains as lively as the day it was written. The story of the High Priest Ryogaku does, for example. Ryogaku had a bad temper; to know him was to dislike him. And Kenko tells this incident about his neighborhood reputation.

"Next to his monastery grew a large nettle-tree, which occasioned the nickname people gave him, the Nettle-tree High Priest. 'That name is outrageous,' said the high priest, and cut down the tree. The stump still being left, people referred to him now as the Stump High Priest. More furious than ever, Ryogaku had the stump dug up and thrown away, but this left a big ditch. People now called him the Ditch High Priest."

If you can resist the brevity, the force, and the implicit moral of that story, then you probably don't need to read Kenko. Go read some naive westerner who spells everything out, like Aesop. But if you enjoy things briefly told, if you want to try the prose equivalent of *waka* and *haiku*, if you already know Montaigne and would like to meet a spiritual kinsman, then you might want to take an evening and read *Essays in Idleness*.

Essays in Idleness.
Kenko. 1332.

31

A Novel About Nirvana

There are odd novels, and then there are very odd novels. Sir Herbert Read's *The Green Child* is one of the very odd ones. It's about nirvana. Nirvana is hard to define, even for Buddhist and Hindu theologians, and harder still to dramatize. The word means "extinguished"—from the Sanskrit verb *nirva*, to be blown out like a candle—and how are you going to write a novel about the state of being blissfully not there? Who wants to be extinguished, anyway? Maybe in the Far East they like the idea, but westerners cling to identity, and read *Self* magazine. Wouldn't such a novel have to be all exotic and oriental, full of holy men in saffron-colored robes and quotations from the Upanishads?

Well, no. There are some other and much more daring options, and Sir Herbert took one of them. Or, rather, he took two of them, because *The Green Child*, though quite a short novel, is in two distinct parts.

The book begins in the mythical South American country of Roncador, a bit over a century ago. Here is the opening sentence:

"The assassination of President Olivero, which took place in the autumn of 1861, was for the world at large one of those innumerable incidents of a violent nature which characterize the politics of the South American continent."

Within a page, one learns that the world at large is quite mistaken. Olivero is not dead at all; for that matter, he's not even South American. He's an Englishman originally named Oliver who has been ruling Roncador for the last 25 years. Or not so much ruling as quietly managing; Roncador is one of the most placid and uneventful of little countries.

Now at the age of fifty Olivero wants to retire from politics and return to England. He has arranged his own apparent assassination, and he travels in a leisurely way to the Yorkshire village where he grew up. The leisureliness is important, because it's the first sign of that abolition of a sense of time which is one of the marks of nirvana. And the faked assassination (easier, I imagine, to carry off in those days before there were CIA agents everywhere)—that's important because it's the first move toward shedding identity.

His first night back in the village—where he remains incognito—Olivero takes a stroll along the little moorland river where he played as a child. Passing a remote mill, he sees in the single lit room an extraordinary sight. A woman in a white dress is tied in a chair, and a man is attempting to force her to drink a cup of warm blood taken from a freshly killed lamb. She is resisting with all her will.

Olivero intervenes. By the next morning, the man is dead, and Olivero and the woman are out on the moors. He has recognized her as Siloen, the Green Child, the surviving one of two very strange children who appeared in the village just at the time he left, thirty years earlier. The man was her husband.

The green children—they have only the faintest green cast to their skin—are like human beings, but without our passionate identity, in fact without passions at all. As you eventually learn, they belong to a race who live in vast caverns under the moors. Siloen and her brother wandered out onto the surface as children, got lost, and so became trapped in our world—that is, the world of hot emotions and husbands and roast beef. As you learn much sooner, the man was forcing her to drink blood in order to keep her alive.

All that is prologue. The two main sections of the book now follow. In the first, Olivero tells Siloen, as they walk on the moors, the story of his long career in Roncador. That story is of life as nearly free of time and selfhood as our race is able to get. Roncador between 1835 and 1860 was a tiny, isolated republic without newspapers or much literacy or a ruling class and almost without change. The Roncadorans farm and keep cattle; they follow the seasons; they like to watch hummingbirds. One year is much like another. It is almost nirvana.

Then, still walking on the moors, Olivero and Siloen find at the source of the little river the hidden entrance to the caverns of her people. They enter nirvana.

Life in the caverns does not involve much self-abnegation, because there is not much self to abnegate. The environment is still more placid and unchanging than that of Roncador, since here there are no seasons. There are just the caves and grottos, perpetually lit with luminesence, perpetually mild, perpetually filled with the music that is one of the two chief arts of the green people.

Cavern life, once you become an adult, falls into four stages. All four are clearly symbolic—as drinking lamb's blood from a cup was also. Siloen's husband may not have been conscious of the parallel with the central Christian rite, whose function is to secure the eternal salvation of the self, but Read certainly was.

In the first stage, you join one of the groups of fifty or so young men and women who go about together, swimming in the warm lakes and gently copulating. (I'm not being clinical, just accurate. I can't use our euphemism of making love, because that fierce, selective passion is unknown.) There being no days, nights, seasons, or clocks, time figures only as the process that imperceptibly lengthens stalactities and ages people.

When one is ready to cease playing—in Olivero's case, quite soon—one joins a work gang. One thus enters the second stage. There are many kinds of gangs: food gatherers, teachers of the young, tenders of the dead, and, highest of all, makers of crystals. Most people sooner or later—how could there be a hurry?—do most kinds of work there are.

Most then go on to the third stage. In that one joins a group of five sages, who walk and talk and think, like the peripatetic philosophers of Athens. And finally, most of the green people become solitary sages, seated in individual grottos, lost in the contemplation of timeless art. That is, listening to the music, looking at the crystals which the best crystal makers bring, hoping to have one accepted by a sage. At death one becomes literally a crystal oneself, through a process of petrifaction. Then nirvana is complete. We see Olivero and Siloen through to that final and eternal stage. They are dead happily ever after, one might say.

There is no obvious moral to *The Green Child*. But there is a curious sense of freedom to the book. Read has done in a different and much more drastic way what Keats did in "Ode on a Grecian Urn." He has abolished the tyranny of time.

Keats did it by a quick-freeze process. The marble youth and maiden on the urn are exempt from age ("For ever wilt thou love, and she be fair!"), but the price they pay is high. As long as the urn lasts, they will be on the verge of kissing each other, but never actually doing so. They exist in an eternity of unfulfilled desire. Olivero and Siloen, on the other hand, have reached a crystal consummation: They are impersonal but complete.

If you want to imagine what it would be like to exist beyond desire, beyond loneliness, and even beyond identity, *The Green Child* is a book to read. And if you want a flaming romance, it most definitely isn't.

The Green Child.
Herbert Read. 1935.

32

In an Offhand Manner

The *New Yorker* once had the official policy of calling its shorter articles "casuals." Or to slip into the style of those articles, the editors had the *habit* of calling them that. "Official" and "policy" are both large earnest words, and they wouldn't fit into the offhand manner of a casual at all.

The offhand manner, the trick of seeming never to take anything quite seriously, the appearance, even, of examining all things quizzically through a monocle—the elegance, in short, of the casual—that was one of the things that first gave The *New Yorker* its reputation. There are even people who think the magazine invented the form.

It didn't, of course. Under various names, the casual essay has been around for a very long time. It has been a particular specialty in England, used and loved by generations of elegant cool-voiced writers. One of the coolest and most elegant was the novelist Rose Macaulay, a member of the same family that a century earlier produced that very uncasual historian Lord Macaulay.

In 1925, shortly before The *New Yorker* was founded, Miss Macaulay published an enchanting book of essays called *A Casual Commentary*. There are about forty essays in it (thirty-nine, if you must know—but it's breaking all the rules of casualness to have counted). Two generations later, most of them remain intensely pleasurable to read. Considering that

Miss Macaulay wrote solely for an English audience, and considering that what she wrote was a series of offhand reflections on events and ideas and even politics of the early 1920s, giving no thought to posterity or high art, and considering that the book is thus both parochial and ephemeral, this is no mean feat.

What keeps the book so readable is, of course, the style. Imagine a cultured Martian visitor writing articles about what she sees on earth. Imagine that Martian with a flawless command of English, a benevolent but wholly detached view of human beings, and no illusions whatsoever. Imagine her a mistress of dry wit. You have something like Rose Macaulay.

Take the several essays she devotes to the British Parliament. None of them is angry or accusatory or anything like that. They are merely cool and devastating.

For example, one of them tells people how to vote—always a handy thing to know in an election year. The historical case is that at the moment she wrote, the Conservative, Liberal, and Labor parties were all vying for power in England. Each claimed, just as political parties do now, that the welfare of the nation, perhaps the country's very survival, depended on its candidates getting into office. Miss Macaulay tended to the opposite view.

"Every now and then," she wrote, "there is a parliamentary election, and then every voter has to decide which of the various candidates who offer themselves as representatives of his constituency he least dislikes, and considers least foolish and useless."

Before the reader even has time to count the number of insults to politicians contained in that suave sentence, she has moved on. "Be sure they will all be quite useless, quite foolish, and quite unable to show any reason why they should represent you. This cannot be helped. Members of Parliament are like that, and that is partly why governments and constitutions are as we see them."

So what's a poor voter to do? Simple. If he or she is especially naive, go for the nearest Reagan-figure. (Miss Macaulay obviously did not use this phrase. Ronald Reagan was a boy of fourteen when the book came out and had not yet been in a single movie or otherwise called himself to her attention. What she did say that translates to Reagan-figure, you will see in a minute.) Other and more sophisticated people should pick the candidate who takes the most stands. Or as Miss Macaulay puts it, "Unless the voter prefers merely to vote for the candidate with the more amiable smile and pleasing address, he had better discover which of them will make the greater number of promises concerning the amelioration of the condition of the constituency. Judicious approach will be found to elicit a remarkable number of these promises from both sides. The promises will not, of course, be kept, but they are good things to have in writing, as they enable the member's constituents to make his parliamentary life a burden to him with reproachful letters."

In another essay she considers the question of what people would really like that politicians and governments can offer. She says (correctly, I think) that most of us are quite unclear: "Vaguely we know that we do not want the politician, that we do want cheap things, no taxes, peace abroad and at home, plenty, a government which interferes with us as little as possible, and no fuss." How to arrange this? Why, by withholding power from everyone—or at least from every public figure. The best thing, she says, would be "to have a House of Commons consisting of three minorities, so that none of them can do anything at all, since we have a well-founded belief that doing is a deadly thing, doing ends in death." She had World War I in mind; among other things, it killed about a quarter of the young men in England, accomplishing no discernible good in the process. An American now can think of Vietnam, Central America, dead Marines in Lebanon, maybe even of the arms race.

But politics are the least of Miss Macaulay's interests. Literature pleased her more, and many of the essays offer advice to writers, to readers, even to journalists. I'm especially fond of an essay she devotes to the aspiring novelist. She has already explained that novels are absurdly easy to write and that they have the great advantage over most kinds of books in that a certain number of people actually read them. Now she is telling the young novelist what to expect after publication day.

"You need not mind what reviews say, for they are not much read except by you and your publishers. But you must make your publishers say, often and conspicuously . . . that your book exists and has sold many copies, for if the general public are told this loudly and often, they hasten to read it; they do not mind whether or not it is good, so long as they believe many others have read it. You must, therefore, make friends with your publisher and get him to proclaim you well. He should, for instance, in public announcements, always add a nought to the number of copies he has sold of your book, so that five hundred has the air of being five thousand, and so forth."

Excellent advice, that, made quaint only by the relative smallness of the numbers. Fortunately, many publishers now seem to be adding two noughts.

But neither politics nor publishing was Rose Macaulay's central interest in *A Casual Commentary*. Women were. She was an early feminist, though obviously never a wild-eyed one, and many of the essays turn on the special interests of women. Housekeeping, for example, and how to get rid of it. Miss Macaulay considers various ways to accomplish this desirable goal, including the currently popular one of turning it over to men. In the end, she has a more radical idea.

"The only solution to this problem which I can suggest— and I hesitate to do it—is, Do *not* keep house. Let the house, or flat, go unkept. Let it go to the devil, and see what happens when it has got there. At the worst, a house unkept cannot be so distressing as a life unlived."

Just for a moment, our Martian was almost serious.

But she soon recovers. Even when there is real injustice to consider, her tone remains casual. It does, for example, in my favorite piece in the whole book: the double essay called "Woman: I. Her Troubled Past," and "Woman: II. Her Dark Future." (The second essay actually considers the future of men as well. "I find it difficult to separate the probable destinies of the two creatures," Miss Macaulay explains.)

If you have a taste for mannered writing, if you are one of those who see that keeping your emotional distance is one of the ways of turning tragedy into comedy and pain into pleasure, Rose Macaulay can hardly fail to delight you. Read *A Casual Commentary*, and then you might even want to try some of her twenty-three novels. I hope you do. I specially recommend *The Towers of Trebizond*. It's the last, best, and wittiest of the lot—the crown of a career that began in 1906 and didn't end until 1956. Indeed, as long as people love casual elegance, it may never end.

> *A Casual Commentary.*
> Rose Macaulay. 1925.

33

Two Hundred One Years Old and Still Impudent

The First Novel about the American Revolution

SCENE: A British warship, HMS *Oddfish*, en route from New York to Rhode Island.

Time: Late fall of 1777.

Characters: Chaptain Furnace commanding *Oddfish*; a passenger, Captain O'Sneak of the British Army; a nameless lieutenant.

The three are discussing the progress of the war against the Americans. Captain Furnace laments General Burgoyne's recent surrender at Saratoga.

THE LIEUTENANT: General Howe's taking Philadelphia is of some advantage, however.

O'SNEAK: He had no business to take it.

THE LIEUTENANT: I think, Captain O'Sneak, it is rather severe to condemn so hastily, before you know the general's reasons, intentions, or indeed any one circumstance of the campaign.

FURNACE: Captain O'Sneak, Captain O'Sneak, I never will allow any degree of censure, while I have the honour very naturally to sit at the head of, or preside at, this table.

O'SNEAK: Sir, I most humbly ask your pardon. I never will take that liberty again.

FURNACE: Never will, Sir, you never shall. G-d strike me dead, if I allow it, by G-d.

O'SNEAK: Sir, I am very sorry—

FURNACE: By G-d, Sir, if you ever *ape* or presume to talk in that way again, I'll turn you neck and heels out of my cabin; and if you do not go quietly, I shall order my sentry to stick his bayonet in your a——; if he refuses, I shall very naturally stick my sword in his.

O'SNEAK: I hope, Sir, you will never have occasion to do that.

What you have just read is a fairly typical scene in a very unusual novel. Considering when it was written, one might even say an extraordinary novel. *The Adventures of Jonathan Corncob* was published in London in 1787. It is one of fewer than a hundred eighteenth-century novels that even refer to the American Revolution. It is one of five written from an American point of view. It is the only comic one. It is, in fact, the *Catch-22* of the Revolution—shorter than Heller's masterpiece, much less sophisticated in terms of technique, but just as full of black humor, and really just as funny.

Jonathan Corncob, the main character and narrator—you could hardly call him the hero—is a Massachusetts farm boy from a Loyalist family. Soon after the book opens, he gets into sexual trouble. There's a girl in the neighborhood named Desire Slawbunk. Her first name doesn't need much comment; her last name does. It's a slight corruption of a word once common in colonial American speech. The early Dutch settlers used to recline on what they called a *slaap bancke*, or sleeping bench. The phrase came into Anglo-colonial slang as "slawbank," still meaning something you lie down on.

"One evening when her father and mother were gone out," Jonathan strolls over to pay Desire a call. In 1988, the two kids might put on a few records and dance, maybe watch some TV. In 1776, they were more apt to bundle, at least in the winter. Bundling, a recognized courtship practice in colonial America, consisted of keeping your clothes on, but getting under a quilt together so as to stay warm, and having a nice chat and maybe a few furtive hugs. Normally the parents would be right there in the room. In many rural houses there *was* only one room.

Jonathan, however, takes full advantage of the fact that Desire's parents are absent. When she becomes pregnant, the town fathers give him the choice of marrying her or paying a fine of fifty pounds. Neither choice appeals to him. Instead he runs off to New York and joins a Loyalist regiment. This particular regiment is not at all prone to pitched battles with Washington's army. Its specialty is stealing cattle from Revolutionary sympathizers in New Jersey and Connecticut.

Later Jonathan serves in the Royal Navy and briefly on an American privateer. He spends several months in an American jail in Boston and several weeks in a British naval hospital in Brooklyn, having contracted veneral disease from the socially pretentious granddaughter of a Presbyterian minister in Manhattan.

This wide range in scenes gives the anonymous author a chance to satirize just about everybody connected with the Revolution on either side. The British naval surgeon in Brooklyn is about as skilled as Captain O'Sneak is brave. Jonathan himself is an even bigger coward than O'Sneak. There's a scene in Boston in which the high-minded patriots decide to find a more or less innocent tea salesman guilty of disloyalty to the rebel cause. There's no particular malice involved, they just want a little excitement. "It was six weeks since the Bostonians had tarred and feathered anybody." The Hessian mercenaries that King George sent over spend most of their time robbing civilians, preying quite impartially on Tories and rebels. As Lieutenant Hastendudenrot says with impeccable logic to a rich American he is about to rob, "If you vas one frynd to the Koning, you vas gif me your vatch; if you vas one repel, by Got I take it." And Hastendudenrot is small potatoes compared to the army and navy suppliers on both sides. Jonathan learns that a weapons contractor who doesn't make at least a hundred thousand pounds for himself on the side is downright incompetent. Some things have not altogether changed.

Along with its obscenity, absurdity, high spirits, and wit,

the book does have a few flaws. The author was clearly an amateur. (From internal evidence I feel pretty sure that his actual occupation was that of a British naval officer, one who had done shore duty as well as sea duty in the colonies, but no one has ever identified him.) Many promising scenes remain undeveloped. The characters are nearly all one-dimensional—which, indeed, tends to be true of absurdist comedy in general. The caricature of colonial American speech patterns is sometimes too broad. Worst of all, the book has no real ending; it simply stops.

That last flaw can be explained if not excused. The author intended to continue Jonathan's adventures later—he says this on the last page. Had he done so, he presumably would have reached some kind of closure. One may safely assume that the reason he didn't is that the book was almost a complete failure. There has never been a second English edition, and the first American edition didn't come out until 1976, 190 years late. Most eighteenth-century Englishmen weren't ready for comedy as black as this. And certainly Americans then weren't ready to see their revolution treated so disrespectfully. Reviewers, as I've noted, complained that Mr. Corncob was excessively bawdy.

The book suits our own time a good deal better. Bawdiness is no barrier now. Absurdism is our native tongue. Post M*A*S*H* and post-Heller, or perhaps one should just say post-Korea and post-Vietnam, reverent views of American wars are no longer required. *The Adventures of Jonathan Corncob* makes the funniest antidote I know to the Revolutionary hagiography most people encounter in school.

The Adventures of Jonathan Corncob,
Loyal American Refugee. 1787.

34

Over Forty and Just Beginning
An Englishwoman's Brilliantly Recorded Life

Only a few totally honest accounts of a human life exist. That's not because people are lacking who would like to tell the truth. (They probably *are* a minority.) It's because you can't tell it unless you know it. Biographers, not being mind readers, never know it all. People who write their own lives are only slightly better off. To see the truth of your own life you must first have gotten beyond all illusions about yourself, and probably about the world as well. Few of us do.

Diana Athill is one of the few. She is also a gifted writer, and, if one may judge by this book, an enchanting woman.

Instead of a Letter is the story of her life up to the age of forty-three. That is, from 1917 to 1960. It is not a typical life. It contains more privilege, more suffering (internal, not imposed), and in the end acuter happiness than is the common lot. And yet, at least to me, it seems like the revelation of a whole sex. Short of being born a woman myself, I don't know where I would get a greater sense of what it would feel like to be female than I did from reading *Instead of a Letter*.

Diana Athill is upper-class English. She grew up mainly in her grandmother's house, which had twenty bedrooms, a park, and a thousand acres of land attached. She loved life there, with its ritual, its servants, even its characteristic English upper-class discomforts, such as no heat. ("'My sponge is *often* frozen solid in the morning,' I remember boasting to some less hardy, less fortunate child.")

At fifteen she fell in love with an Oxford undergraduate named Paul, who had come to the estate to tutor her brother. At nineteen she became engaged to him. They also began to sleep together, a more unusual event in 1936 than it might be now. A couple of years later, soon before they were to be married, he broke the engagement in a way so cruel that it caused her to lose all confidence in herself. (He didn't *mean* to be cruel; he was just the sort of man who hates awkward scenes.)

For the next twenty years she led a kind of half-life: plenty of affairs that were sure to lead nowhere; a successful career, but she often slept twelve hours a night on weekends to be rid of the time; a general sense of waiting, but of waiting for nothing in particular except the slow arrival of old age.

And then at forty-one, a miraculous reversal. Having almost by chance started to write stories, she entered a contest, and she won it. Soon after, she began her first serious relation with a man since she was twenty-two. The book ends on a high note.

Here, in short, is the plot of many a romance novel. Here is a life begun in joy, brought to sorrow, and then when least expected returned to joy. The chief difference is that in the romance it would have returned about fifteen years sooner, while she was still able to have children and a long, long future.

So where do the honesty and the overwhelming sense of female life come in? Under the plot. In the details of the plot.

Take, for example, the night that Paul first kissed her. She was barely seventeen, he a very sophisticated twenty-one. They happened to meet at a dance where each had gone with a group of other people. She knew plenty of boys her own age. "I never thought of holding them off for Paul's sake; the gaining of experience was too valuable and exciting in itself to be rejected. He was the man I loved, he was the man I was waiting for, but meanwhile if anyone else wanted to fall in love with me, or to kiss me, or to tell me I was attractive, I would welcome it greedily. It was pure chance that it was, in fact, Paul who kissed me first. By then I had been waiting for him for two years, which anyone over 25 should read as five, or eight, or ten."

Paul perceives her readiness, spends the evening with her, eventually takes her out to his car. "When he turned my face up and kissed me on the mouth, we were both surprised: I because his lips were cold and a little sticky whereas I had expected them to be warm and smooth; he because mine were hot and parted whereas he had expected them to be like a child's. He told me later that he had thought, 'The little devil, she has been at it already, this is not the first time,' but it was."

When Paul brings her home, very late, her mother is still awake, and furious. Under cross-questioning, she admits to having been kissed.

"'Oh,' she said, and I could sense the clutch of fear in her stomach, 'Did he just kiss you, or did he—are you sure he didn't *mess you about?*'"

"I could not strike her because she was in bed and I was standing some paces away. I could only mutter savagely 'How could you say that!' and slam out of her room thinking, 'Damn her, damn her, damn her!' I could still feel Paul's dinner jacket against my cheek, those surprising lips, and his hand lightly on my breast where my own hand held it; I was still wrapped about with *the most important moment of my life*, and she had said 'mess you about.'"

Then she ends the chapter, "Poor parents, what are they to do?"

I'm afraid one example won't convey the marvelous frankness and immediacy of this book, let alone the calm wisdom with which Diana Athill at forty-three looks back on her life and understands its every nuance. There is no room to quote the fifty or so other examples I would like to, such as her account of her first wartime job in England, or her wonderful analysis of a Greek man with whom she doesn't have an affair on Corfu, or her relation to rooms in which she lives and how she decides when it's worth keeping them neat and when it's not. About all I can do is say there were more than fifty times I sighed with pleasure at how well this woman writes, how acutely she perceives.

Not everyone, I admit, responds to the book as I do. When it first came out in London in 1962, the reviewer in the *Times* of London (anonymous in those days) was appalled. Admitting the brilliance of the writing, he deplored the honesty: "She will either horrify or embarrass those readers who believe in the desirability of clinging to some shred of reticence."

But that was in another country, and long ago. I think most American readers now will find the book pure joy. Their one complaint is apt to be that the account stops short in the middle of Ms. Athill's life. And even to that there is an answer. In 1986, she published *After a Funeral*. It's no sequel, being focused entirely on one strange episode of her later life. Neither is it quite so good a book as *Instead of a Letter*, though equally free from shreds of reticence. But it's quite good enough to go on to, as one might from Miss Austen to Miss Eden.

Instead of a Letter.
Diana Athill, 1962.

35

The Best of All Imaginary Islands

Cult books come and cult books go—that's part of what it means to be a cult book. A few keep reappearing, however. They get discovered over and over by successive waves of admirers. After the third or fourth reappearance, the suspicion begins to arise that this isn't a cult book, after all. It's a masterpiece with problems.

Islandia is such a book. This obscure novel, the lifework of a man who wasn't even a professional writer, has had a devoted following for forty-five years. It has gone out of print numerous times, and always triumphantly returned. Some of its admirers would emigrate in a minute to the country where the story takes place, if only they could find it. Others know the book very nearly by heart, even though it's a thousand pages long. All this spells "cult."

That *Islandia* is also a masterpiece is what I'm about to argue. And that it has problems, no one who learns the plot is likely to dispute.

Islandia began as the fantasy world of a small boy named Austin Tappan Wright, around the year 1890. In the beginning it was a fairly commonplace fantasy world. The little boy imagined an island kingdom. There people rode horses from castle to castle, instead of taking trains from city to city as his actual family did. (His actual family was quite high powered and very modern. The father was dean of the Harvard graduate school, the mother a novelist.)

Many children have such fantasy worlds, and most abandon them at the beginning of adolescence. Wright did not. He grew up to be a distinguished professor of law, a husband, a father, all of that—but he continued to live part time in Islandia.

As he grew, so did his imaginary world. It ceased to be an island and became the southernmost and coldest part of the Karain continent, somewhere below the equator. It kept its king, but he became very much a constitutional monarch, not an absolute ruler. It dropped the castles. It kept the horses—but they were no longer part of the romantic imaginings of a small boy. They were part of the utopian vision of a fully mature man, one who has thought out the relationship between speed of travel and meaning of journey. It gathered a two-thousand-year history, a complete sociology, a stunning cast of characters, a theory of how human beings can best lead satisfying lives. In the end, *Islandia* became the best vision I know of a life in which high culture coexists with low technology—and with no help from the goddess Mari, or any other god or goddess.

The story the book tells is vastly too complicated to summarize. I can give some indication of how it begins, though. It begins with a young Harvard student, John Lang. In his freshman year, which is 1901, he meets an extraordinary and charismatic classmate named Dorn, said to be from the hermit kingdom of Islandia. Little is known about this remote country, because almost no one has been there. Islandia expelled Saracen invaders in the twelfth century, Christian missionaries in the sixteenth, and ever since a British attempt to establish treaty ports in the 1840s, it has had a law permitting only a hundred foreigners in the country at any one time. Tourism does not exist, and there is no Baedeker.

Dorn and Lang become friends, and the American winds up learning a great deal about Islandia: its farm economy, its small size (the population is just over 2.2 million), its unusual theories about the relation between mind and body. He even begins to learn the language. Not long after Lang graduates, there is a fresh attempt by the great powers to compel Islandia to enter the modern world as defined by them. Under gunboat pressure, Islandia agrees to accept diplomatic representatives from the major countries on a temporary basis. Partly because he knows more about Islandia than most Americans, and partly because he has a rich and influential uncle who means to use him as a cat's paw in getting trade concessions, Lang becomes the first U.S. consul in Islandia.

Two plots now move forward simultaneously. One tells the story of Islandia itself over the next two years. That tiny country has to decide whether to yield itself up for development or to keep its own way of life, even at the risk of destruction. This is a thrilling story, thrillingly told. People who advocate development will find it so, just as much as those who don't. Among its other virtues, *Islandia* is a page-turner.

The second plot is John Lang's personal story. Here the book is mainly about love. Lang is twenty-four when he becomes U.S. consul, and he is emotionally an intense person. During the course of the book he has three great romances, two with Islandian girls and one with an American. This last begins when he is back home for a time, having ignominiously lost his diplomatic post. He failed to please his uncle and the other powerful businessmen who wanted the Islandian coal and copper.

Islandians have very different views about love than Americans do. So different that they have to use three terms instead of our one. Love takes the forms of *alia*, *ania*, and *apia*. Partly because it's hard to do out of context, and partly in the hope of making you so curious you'll read the book, I shall define none of the three—except to say that *apia* has a diminutive form, *apiata*, and *that* corresponds to the English word "lust," though lacking the pejorative connotation.

Few people have been better than Austin Wright at dramatizing the nuances of the various emotions we lump together as "love," and in this way, too, the book is a masterpiece.

But there is still one plot element I haven't mentioned. It is this one that makes *Islandia* a masterpiece with problems. The kingdom of Islandia faces other threats besides those of European colonization and American exploitation. There are also wild tribesmen who live across the mountains, right there in the Karain continent. They're called the Bants; they've recently been armed by the Germans (who have established a protectorate in part of northern Karain), and they love to come over the mountains and raid Islandia.

No harm so far. That just makes for more excitement. The problem is that while the Islandians are white, civilized, and very appealing, the Bants are black, uncivilized, and fairly awful. It makes a reader uncomfortable.

And yet—this is a book I have taught to college classes that included black students. They were not thrilled at the role played by the Bants, but some of them liked *Islandia* itself very much. All, I think, conceded that Wright's focus was not on racial prejudice. He wanted a danger over the mountains. In the end it wouldn't change the book much if it were black Islandians threatened by white Bants. Furthermore, race in the genetic sense is simply not his concern. You learn in the course of the book that the Islandians were once scattered in tiny groups all over the Karain, and only coalesced into a nation after the Bants arrived. Written records do not go back that far, but present-day Islandians take for granted that their ancestors include some of the early invading Bants. This is a world that Austin Wright invented, and if he had wanted racial purity, he could easily have had it. Obviously he didn't.

But it's not for the Bant wars that one would read *Islandia* in any case. One would read it partly for the great vision of what life would be like if there were no rat race and no fast lane. And one would read it partly for the characters. There are about a dozen who are not only three-dimensional but damn near four. That gives them two and a half more dimensions than characters in utopian novels generally have. To us in the cult, these characters are unforgettable. I think they would be to anybody.

Islandia.
Austin Tappan Wright, 1942.

36

A C. S. Lewis Miscellany

C. S. Lewis is not an obscure writer. Half the children in this country have read his *Chronicles of Narnia*—or at least seen a TV special based on them. A quarter of the adults have read *The Screwtape Letters*—or at least heard of it. Ninety-nine percent of the Renaissance scholars know Lewis's magisterial *English Literature in the Sixteenth Century, Excluding Drama.*

But Lewis was so multitalented, so various in what he did, that there are books of his almost no one knows about. Wonderful books. One of them is called *They Asked for a Paper.*

In no way is it a probable book. It's a collection of occasional pieces he wrote over a period of twenty years—and *that's* usual enough. Every journalist who ever wrote a few dozen articles dreams of seeing the best of them collected between hard covers, and a good many achieve this dream. Clive James, the English critic, has made books out of his comments on TV shows.

But these books and their contents are like eggs in an egg carton or wine bottles in a case. The contents match. *This* volume is humorous newspaper columns, *that* one is political essays. Heloise's is household hints.

C. S. Lewis's is rather more miscellaneous. *They Asked for a Paper* contains twelve pieces. The first, and my favorite, is the inaugural lecture he gave at Cambridge when that university succeeded in luring him from Oxford with a newly created chair. The last is a sermon he preached (as a layman, he was not in orders) at the Church of Saint Mary the Virgin in Oxford. In between come all sorts of things. There's a "toast"—a spectacularly long one, it runs to four thousand words—he gave at the annual dinner of the Sir Walter Scott Club of Edinburgh. Let others read scholarly articles on Scott or consult encyclopedias; standing up at that dinner, Lewis gave the best short account of who Scott was and why he matters that I have seen.

There's a paper he read at Westfield College (part of the University of London) back in 1941. It is called "Psycho-Analysis and Literary Criticism," and it is a masterpiece. It begins with the twenty-third of Freud's *Introductory Lectures*, the one in which Freud argued that art is compensatory fantasy. Lewis does not attack Freud—whose work he knows well, as he knew most major writing. He has no wish to attack a great pioneer. He merely shows that Freud's vision is incomplete.

There is no space here to summarize twenty pages of argument as densely packed as if it were by Saint Thomas Aquinas. But I will just mention two points. Lewis makes a wonderfully useful distinction between two kinds of things that can happen when you get absorbed in a novel. One is called low identification. It's when you as your own real self identify with a character in the novel. You're a boy of sixteen; you identify with the dashing teenage hero. You're a Chinese girl; you identify with the gorgeous oriental heroine. The whole point is that if you were only smarter, richer, luckier, but still you, you might actually be that character in the book.

The other, of course, is called high identification, and now in reading you utterly forget who you are. As a boy of sixteen, you may identify with a talking dragon, even though there is no possible way you could ever be a dragon, and even if you were, you wouldn't be the elderly female dragon with green scales that your disembodied consciousness has identified with. It is high identification, Lewis brilliantly shows, that Freud's theory does not adequately deal with.

The other point I can take time for begins with a summary of Freud's Tenth Introductory Lecture, the one in which Freud sets out the concept of universal symbols. In every subconscious, he says, journeys stand for death, gardens and flowers for the female body, and so on. Lewis quotes Freud's famous question: "Does it not begin to dawn upon us that the many fairy tales which begin with the words 'once upon a time there were a king and queen' simply mean 'once upon a time there were a father and mother'?" And then he is able to show that no, the fairy tales don't *simply* mean that, which is to say, that and nothing more. They mean that plus much else. He is especially brilliant when he brings Freudian (and Jungian) symbols up against that great medieval poem *The Romance of the Rose*, where already the guarded garden stands for the female body, and the rose itself for the flower of virginity, and the thirteenth-century French authors knew that—it was the concept they built the poem on—but went far beyond it.

If *I* had twenty pages available, I would love to report what Lewis told the British Academy about Hamlet when they invited him to give the annual Shakespeare lecture. And because nothing else I've read about Kipling has an insight so interesting as the one Lewis offered the English Association in an address to them, I'd like to put in a word about that. Most of all, I'd like to reprint word for word his inaugural lecture at Cambridge, called "De Descriptione Temporum." (The rest is in English.) Lewis came to hold the new chair in

Medieval and Renaissance Literature. This gave him a reason to talk about historical periods, what they are and what they mean, starting with the Dark Ages. Robert Frost wrote a poem called "The Lesson for Today," in which he imagines a court poet in ninth-century France speaking to the poets of today on the same subject. That's the only comparable work I know that has even nearly the same power to move as Lewis's lecture. And Frost, of course, did not have Lewis's incredible learning.

I do have space to say one last thing. I dare to recommend Lewis in his scholarly role to the general reader because he is that rarity among great scholars, a person with a clear and extremely readable prose style. Other scholars have sometimes called him *too* clear, meaning they think he oversimplifies. And I confess that occasionally, like Saint Thomas Aquinas, he will by sheer force of logic make what seems to be an overwhelming point; later, looking back, one suspects the evidence has been forced into a neater pattern than complex truth will bear.

But mostly Lewis is amazing in his ability to express the full complexity of a thing in language as clear and ringing as crystal.

They Asked for a Paper.
C. S. Lewis. 1962.

37

A Girl, a Horse—and for Once a Good Book

There are well over a thousand horse books in print in this country, ranging from *Equine Hoof Care* to *Black Beauty*.

A surprising number of them fit in one narrow category: the horse-and-girl novel intended for feminine readers between the ages of about nine and fifteen. Most of them are pretty feeble stuff—as, indeed, are most of the books in any *any* category, up to and including epic poetry. (Take a look at some of the early American epics, such as Joel Barlow's *Columbiad*, if you're in any serious doubt.)

But horsy novels for the younger set tend to be specially shoddy, just like first-kiss novels, diet books, computer guides—all the sorts of books that get written primarily to tap a market rather than to say something an author wants badly to say.

Born to Race is one of the occasional exceptions. In form it is like many another: The main characters are a thirteen-year-old girl named Suzy Taylor and a horse named Whickery. The setting is a horse farm in Virginia. The action consists primarily of Suzy riding horses, feeding horses, solving mysteries, outthinking her father and his head stableman, eventually getting to go to the Kentucky Derby and getting to see Whickery win it.

But three things distinguish it, maybe four. One is the author's passion for her subject. Cherry Hill Farm, where Suzy Taylor and Whickery both live, is a stud farm—that is, Suzy's father raises thoroughbreds, and races them. Unlike the large majority of people who do this, Mr. Taylor actually makes his living at it. He's no safe millionaire with a hobby. When he has a disastrous year at the track, as he does in the early part of this book, he is in real danger of losing farm, horses, and everything.

This setting was not something the author picked because she figured it was good saleable stuff. It was in her bones. She grew up in rural Virginia. Long ago she had cousins who *did* have such a racing stable and who after enough disastrous years lost farm, horses, everything. Still more, she had a brother who went north and made sufficient money in New York to buy back one of the lost farms—where he promptly set to breeding race horses. His great Derby winner was Secretariat. This farm and these horses she knew well, and that knowledge informs, and fills, and floods through *Born to Race*. One thing that distinguishes the book is truth.

Another is a kind of feminism that I'm not sure the author was fully conscious of. After all, the book came out in 1959, well before the present feminist movement began.

It is not simply that Suzy Taylor catches the grain thief that neither her father nor Ben, the head stableman, was able to. (She does it more by persistence than brilliance, which is part of the truth of the book.) It's not just that Whickery is a filly, a young female horse, rather than a colt, even though in every year but two colts have won the Derby. It's the little semiconscious details.

For example, like most thoroughbreds Whickery is highstrung. A male observer who wished to be objectionable might even say she has a tendency to get hysterical. In the real world of racing it is the custom to surround tense thoroughbreds with much calmer animals, and so it is in the book. But there is an interesting gender twist. First Whickery is given what amounts to a pet dog to live in her box stall with her, a young male Dalmatian named Jo-Boy. When she travels (to race-tracks), a placid male lead-pony named Sir Knight goes along. And finally she has her personal goat, inevitably named Billy, who shares one corner of the stall with Jo-Boy. One female, with three male attendants, not even counting the human grooms.

There is a moment when Billy, full of male arrogance, starts to snatch a bite of hay from Whickery's very mouth. She nips him hard. In revenge he tries to butt her. Ben, the head stableman, instantly ties him in his corner, over the protests of Suzy, who points out that Whickery has given him a quite painful bite and maybe has the butt coming. "'Miss Whickery,' said Ben, ' is going to be one of the best race horses in the country. . . . Mr. Billy is just common, ordinary goat.'" And, Ben adds, "'He'll lose his stable job if he tries any butting.'"

This is not a book that keeps women in their place—at least, if their place is anywhere but at the top.

The third distinguished thing about the book is as old-fashioned as the feminism is modern. There is a code of behavior that nearly all the characters accept. Its main tenets are: don't cheat, don't borrow, don't complain.

For example, Suzy is in anguish when it becomes definite that Whickery will run in the Derby, because she won't be able to watch. She is too young legally to be at a race track. She briefly has a fantasy about cutting her hair short and going to Kentucky disguised as a stable boy. "'I know enough about horses to do the work,'" she argues. "'You do,' said her father irritably, 'but you don't seem to know much about honor.'"

She does, of course; her father was just being cross. How she gets honorably and publicly into the stands is a wonderful story—the best and the most moving section of the book.

Or again, in this age of planned deficits, the book's view of debt is old-fashioned, rather pleasingly so. When Whickery begins to win major stakes races, Mr. Taylor is finally able to begin paying off his bank loan. Suzy doesn't worry that he may be losing a nice tax shelter by doing this. "Not to owe! Why, we'd be, we'd be *free*, Suzy thought. Our barn would really be our barn, and our farm *ours*."

Without ever preaching, and without pretending the costs of decent behavior are lower than they are, the book shows us human beings one can admire.

Finally, the book has true emotional power. There are three scenes where tears of pride come to one's eyes, or at least to my eyes. The last of them, at Churchill Downs, is a stunner.

Admittedly, I may be partial. I have never written about a book by my mother before, and fondness for her memory may blind me a little. But only a little. I can still see the book's faults clearly: the one small inconsistency in plot, the underdeveloped characters of Suzy's best friend and of her mother, the awkward time jump from when Whickery is two to when she is three and eligible for the Derby. I am clear it is a good book, not a great one. I'm also clear it's good enough to give real pleasure to any horse-struck daughter, or even son.

Born to Race,
Blanche C. Perrin. 1959.

38

A Genius Grew in Brooklyn

In 1935, to rapturous cries from the reviewers, Clarence Day published a book about his nineteenth-century childhood. He called it *Life With Father*. Father was a self-confident, pre-Freudian New Yorker—a wealthy stock broker utterly untroubled by doubts of any sort. To be part of his household was sort of like living with an affectionate steamroller. To be his eldest son was to have the steamroller always flatten your patch of street first. Day made the most of this situation, combining insight and high comedy. The public loved it.

Success breeds followers. The next year another book about a steamroller childhood came out. This one was called *A Genius in the Family*. Once again, the author was an eldest son. Once again the central character was a self-confident, pre-Freudian father, this one named Hiram Maxim. (Later he became Sir Hiram, when he got mad at the U.S. Government and moved to England.)

Who needs *two* books about dominant WASP fathers in late nineteenth-century New York? Well, as it happens, anyone who enjoys good reading does. Hiram Maxim, Jr., doesn't write nearly as well as Clarence Day, Jr., but he has the same total recall of his childhood. He has as keen a sense of the ridiculous—and he has even richer material to work with. Father Day was a normal Victorian writ large: a well-bred

New York businessman in a tall silk hat, self-assured enough to allow his eccentricities free play, but underneath made of the same kind of flesh as the rest of us.

Father Maxim, though he too wore a tall silk hat, and must have looked quite similar when he walked down the street in Brooklyn, differed a lot from most people. To begin with, he really was a genius, and of one of the more picturesque varieties. He was a mad-genius inventor. He made a fortune with the Maxim machine gun, almost beat Edison to the electric light, spent much of the 1890s building steam-powered airplanes. These matters concerned him; most aspects of everyday life did not. Even more than Mr. Day, Mr. Maxim was unselfconscious about his behavior.

For example, in the very respectable part of Brooklyn where he and his family lived, it was customary to have a tiny lawn in front of your house. To protect the grass, you put up a heavy cast-iron fence with a heavy cast-iron gate in it. This you had pull open and swing shut each time you went in or out. Only not Mr. Maxim. He was always in a hurry. And in his top hat and dignified Prince Albert coat he would vault over the gate.

What really set him apart, though, were his persistence and his odd, almost inhuman sense of humor. As to persistence, how many people, after being robbed in Paris, would routinely scan crowds ever after, just in case they might spot one of the robbers? Or having against all odds actually spotted one—in England, thirteen years later—would compel a couple of Scotland Yard detectives to join them in a stake-out, and keep the poor cops there two full days? Or, having got the robber arrested, would drop all other business and spend a month in French courts making sure he also got convicted?

Father Maxim was prepared to put that kind of effort into almost anything, including his jokes. Take the case of the

counterfeit penny. When little Hiram was about four he con-
ceived a passion for a small white dog owned by the neighborhood druggist in Brooklyn. One day he got carried away and
asked if the druggist would give him the dog. What he got was
a wise-guy city answer. Sure, sonny, bring me a two-headed
penny and I'll give you the dog.

At least in 1873, four-year-olds were naive. Little Hiram
hurried home and asked his mother to check all her pennies,
in case she had a two-headed one. They don't exist, she told
him. But trusting the druggist (and wanting the dog), he
wouldn't believe her. When his father came home, same
question but different response. Father Maxim goes through
all his pennies twice, seems surprised that none has two
heads, says there are sure to be two-headed ones over in
Manhattan. He'll look tomorrow.

What he actually does the next day is to suspend his research for the United States Electric Light Company and
spend the morning making one. That night he pretends to
have forgotten the whole thing and is startled when little
Hiram goes through his pockets and sure enough finds a two-
headed penny. (The druggist is dumfounded when *he* sees it,
but does not yield the dog.)

That joke was kindly. So, more or less, was the one where
Father Maxim assures his young son that the barren peach
tree in the back yard will yield a bountiful and quite speedy
crop if fertilized with a dead cat. (Dead cat? Right. Street
cleaning was not elaborate in the 1870s, and with a little
looking a boy could expect to find almost any kind of debris,
if not in the gutter than in some vacant lot.) Little Hiram duly
locates a long-dead cat, and plants it under the tree. Within
twenty-four hours the tree is glorious with fruit. It's the full
bushel of store-bought peaches his father has painstakingly
tied to the branches.

But the hot poker trick was not kindly. Like many prosperous New York families in the 1870s, the Maxims had an Irish cook. It amused Father Maxim to test on her the claim he had read that extreme heat and extreme cold feel the same to human touch. He chilled a poker, announced that it was white hot, and advanced on the cook. She was completely taken in, and when the poker touched her, she fainted. As soon as she recovered consciousness and some degree of coherence, she quit, "declaring she would not remain with a family where the man of the house branded the servants on their necks." Of course there was no brand.

As his son tells the story, Sir Hiram was not conscious of the cruelty involved. He just had an original mind and a complete willingness to use people experimentally. Hard on the cook in that case, wonderful for his daughter Florence in another case. When little Florence first encountered arithmetic in school, she couldn't seem to grasp it. After some weeks, her teacher announced that she was mentally retarded and never *would* grasp it. Teachers ought to know. Nevertheless, that same evening her indignant father invented a new and very odd way to teach arithmetic, tried it out on his daughter, discovered by her bedtime that he could teach her more in one session than her class had learned all fall. She never had trouble with math again.

Hiram Maxim was a true original. Hiram, Jr., was not a true writer—he preferred designing automobiles and gun silencers—but he rose to his subject. The book is not profound and never aimed to be, and yet it has a kind of wisdom along with its hundred wonderful stories. *A Genius in the Family* is worth a few rapturous cries.

A Genius in the Family.
Hiram P. Maxim. 1936.

Huck Finn's French Counterpart

Was there ever a French equivalent of Huckleberry Finn? Yes, as it happens, there was. The equivalence isn't exact, because turn-of-the-century France and nineteenth-century Missouri were extraordinarily different places. Furthermore, the French boy really existed, while Huck came mostly from Mark Twain's imagination. But there's still enough overlap to make Marcel Pagnol's memoirs of his childhood in Provence even more interesting to an American than they would be to, say, an Egyptian or a Czech.

Marcel Pagnol, who grew up to be one of France's great filmmakers, was born in a little town near Toulon, but spent his childhood in Marseilles. His father taught grade school; his pretty young mother had been a seamstress. When Marcel was eight, his parents rented an old farmhouse in a remote mountain village, to use for the summer holidays. It's at this point that Marcel (who is going to play a role somewhat like that of Tom Sawyer) meets his Huck—a peasant boy from the village, named Lili. The city-bred son of the atheist schoolmaster and the superstitious Provençal farmboy become instant friends.

Most of that first summer they spend in the woods. They snare birds, they explore caves, they retrieve game for Marcel's father and uncle (who have come to the village partly for the hunting). It is a true rural idyll, lovingly remembered by Marcel Pagnol in his old age. It is also wonderfully funny. Pagnol was famous in his films for humor without malice, and so it is in this book.

Finally, there are the astonishing (and, I think, unconscious) parallels with Tom and Huck. Like Tom, Marcel Pagnol is bookish. Tom has read all those Gothic romances, and adores the idea of knights and dungeons; Marcel has read James Fenimore Cooper, and adores the idea of Indians. He would like to be one, preferably a Comanche. He has also read authors like Voltaire with his father and is proud of his enlightenment. Like Huck, Lili knows nothing of literature. He just knows the Provençal landscape the way Huck knows the river, and Provençal folk culture the way Huck knows that of the American south.

There's a scene, for example, where they see a huge flock of starlings. Lili, ever practical, is wishing they could catch about fifty of them to sell for a franc apiece. Marcel is more interested in starling theory.

"'Uncle Jules told me they can be tamed. . . . '"

"'Of course,' Lili said. 'My brother had a tame one. And he talked, too, but only in dialect.'"

"'Oh, but I'd teach them French,' I said. [As distinct, he means, from the patois of the village.]

"'I'm not so sure they'd learn it,' Lili observed, 'because they're country birds, you see. . . . '" Score one for Lili.

Or there'll be a scene at night. It is the end of summer, and Marcel is running away. He doesn't want to return to Marseilles and school. He wants to stay in the mountains forever, and catch birds, and be wild. Lili is guiding him through the dark woods to a secret cave where he is initially going to hide out. They see some sort of moving shadow, and Lili is very frightened because he thinks it's the ghost of Big Felix, a shepherd who was murdered fifty years before. Marcel is frightened too, but merely because he is eight years old and in a very dark wood at night. Even in his fear he remembers his father's teaching, and loftily assures Lili that there are no such things as ghosts. Uncle Jules (who works in the prefectural office in Marseilles, and is therefore a very important man) doesn't believe in them either.

" 'They laugh at ghosts, [Marcel says]. And me too, I laugh at them. That's what I do. Yes, LAUGH AT THEM!"

" 'Well, they don't make my father laugh, because he's seen the ghost, he has. He's seen it four times."

" 'Your father's a good sort, but he can't even read!"

" 'I'm not saying he can read, I'm saying he's *seen* it!' "

Score another for Lili, who goes on triumphantly to tell Marcel how to deal with ghosts by his father's method, which is to threaten them with "four signs of the cross and six kicks up the arse."

Though usually printed together, *My Father's Glory* and *My Mother's Castle* are actually two separate books—short ones, about 175 pages each. They're the first two of a series of four that Pagnol wrote under the general title *Memories of Childhood*. (So he wrote in French, and the real title is *Souvenirs de l'enfance*. Let's not get picky. Anyway, the translation by Rita Barisse is so good that one just doesn't worry about the language of origin.)

Young Marcel's adventures with Lili are by no means the sole theme. In the first volume, Pagnol concentrates on the hunting rivalry between his father and Uncle Jules, and he makes it into a sort of daguerreotype album come alive. There were numerous moments during the hunting excursions, and also after the father's triumph, when the only reason I didn't hug myself for pleasure is that I have never figured out how to do that. If M. Pagnol had been present, I would certainly have given *him* a congratulatory Gallic hug.

Even in the second volume, Lili shares honors with a series of great landowners and their employees. There is a complicated and most un-Missouri-like reason for this. By the second year, the Pagnols are going to their mountain retreat every weekend. First they take a train out from Marseilles. Then they walk four hours to the village. They are heavily laden, because they are too poor to own separate cooking vessels, etc., for the two houses, and many bulky things get carried back and forth.

As the starling flies, the distance from where they leave the train up to the village is not great—but the road takes a huge detour to go around four consecutive chateaux. It happens that a small irrigation canal runs through the four estates, though, and it further happens that the canal keeper was once a student of Marcel's father. He insists on letting them shortcut through the estates (it saves them two hours of walking, each way). Eventually he gives them an official government key that opens the canal gates, and each weekend they scurry through without even the keeper's company. Both parents worry all the time—the mother because what they're doing is illegal (and some of these owners are *counts*), the father because he is violating his own principles.

Eventually, of course, they are spotted—and not just by one person but by several guards and tenant farmers and by one owner. The various responses are intensely French. Comte Jean de X, the old colonel of cuirassiers, is courtliness personified, especially to the pretty young mother. Binucci, head guard for the Baron des Actes, is a sadist, but a thoroughly bureaucratic one who immediately begins to write the report that he hopes will cause father Pagnol to lose his job. (He is foiled by the brilliant bureaucratic counterstokes of the canal keeper.) Dominique, the tenant farmer on a third estate, plays charades. They're designed to make his master think he's persecuting the Pagnols while actually out of feelings of fraternité and egalité he's befriending them. These are sweet if occasionally sentimental scenes. The whole book has a kind of sweetness.

And yet, France *is* different. American readers of Pagnol need to be warned about one thing. It was normal practice in Provençe in 1903 to eat songbirds, as it still is in southern Italy. Larks, warblers, thrushes, the characters devour them all. There are certain chapters I cannot honestly recommend to members of the Audubon Society. But the book as a whole— only hearts of stone would fail to love it.

My Father's Glory and *My Mother's Castle*.
Marcel Pagnol. 1960.

Tanya Must Die

Of major living Russian writers, Arkady and Boris Strugatsky are perhaps the least known in America. There are numerous reasons, most of them bad.

One is that they write science fiction. Many, perhaps even most serious readers, intellectuals, persons of letters disdain science fiction. Knowing what is true—that throughout its hundred-year history, most science fiction has been tripe, and poorly written tripe at that—they have simply dismissed the genre. (Some of them make an exception for Ray Bradbury, a curious choice. He is actually minor as a science fiction writer, though a fine and fancy stylist.) They have no idea that there are a handful of writers, such as Ursula LeGuin, Walter Miller, E. M. Forster (in his 1904 novella *The Machine Stops*) and the brothers Strugatsky, whose work will be deeply interesting even to people who ordinarily spurn science fiction. One reason the Strugatskys are little known is that they are victims of this prejudice.

Another is that they do not fit comfortably into either of the categories that most Americans have in their minds for Soviet writers. We tend to think that a Soviet writer is either going to be a heroic dissident, who at terrible personal risk writes against the regime, or a slavish party hack who turns out "socialist realism." We cherish the dissidents and generally ignore the party liners.

The Strugatskys are neither. They are Russians who love Russia, communists who believe (mostly) in communism. But they also believe in independent thought, the right if not the actual duty of all people to keep a critical eye on their governments. They are not unlike the sort of American who, loving this country and wishing to live nowhere else, nevertheless thinks we are horribly wrong in our policy toward Central America, insane to contemplate Star Wars—and freely says so. The Strugatskys, living under a more repressive rule, are less free to speak plainly. They nevertheless convey their criticism clearly enough so that at least twice books of theirs have been suppressed. But they themselves remain fully accepted. For example, in 1981 they jointly won the Aelita Prize, given by the Union of Soviet Writers. We have no place in our mythology for such people.

The third reason that so few Americans know the Strugatskys is the saddest of all. Their work is almost unobtainable here. That's not because it hasn't been translated. To my knowledge, thirteen of their books exist in English translation—some in more than one version. All thirteen have been published in the United States—some by more than one publisher. How many of them could you go out tomorrow morning and buy? One. The novel called *Escape Attempt*. It's worth reading, too, but it is not one of their very best. Their very best are the novella *Far Rainbow*, the great interconnected set of stories published as *Noon: 22nd Century*, and the strange novel, set in Canada, called *Roadside Picnic*. You'd have to go to England to buy even one of these three; the other two can't be had at all. A pity that most publishers casually treat major literature like hula hoops or pet rocks.

Far Rainbow is for me the most moving of all the Strugatskys' work. Only the first time I read it was I actually crying at the end (an effect a book produces on me maybe once in five years). But both other times I still felt joyous and sad and wrung out, as if I had finally come to understand what Aristotle meant by catharsis.

The story takes place two or three centuries from now on a remote and beautiful planet called simply Rainbow. Only about a thousand people live on Rainbow, and nearly all the grownups are scientists. The whole planet constitutes a research center where physicists are attempting to perfect zero-transport, or the instantaneous transmission of matter across space. They have reached the point where they can send objects but not yet living beings. (Without killing them, that is.) Eight highly trained pilots have been on the planet for the last three years, waiting to be the first people sent.

The novel doesn't begin with anything about zero-transport, however. It begins with a love scene. A young physicist named Robert Sklyarov and a teacher from Children's Colony named Tanya are sitting outside his observation post at night, talking as lovers do. That dialogue alone, perfectly capturing the intimacy of two people who feel totally secure with each other, is worth reading the book for.

You do get a hint of zero-physics, though, in the middle of the scene. While Tanya is there, Robert must dash back into his lab for a minute to answer a routine phone call from another physicist-observer. There had been a transmission of matter the previous day—and always, when matter is sent, a tremendous shock wave comes down Rainbow from the poles toward the equator. Once, seven years ago, that wave got out of control and destroyed a considerable slice of the planet. Since then, many new safety and control measures have been taken, and they are effective. Robert and the man who called are just doing standard tracking of the current wave.

The scene now shifts to the scientific village on the equator which is also the political capital of Rainbow. Morning has come, and it's a busy day. A happy one too. A small starship has arrived with much-needed lab equipment, and there is a wonderful, funny scene at the spaceport, as representatives of many labs try to outmaneuver each other and resort to outright deception in the effort to get their share and perhaps a bit more than their share of the new supplies.

This same day is also when Children's Colony (away from the equator in a cooler spot) is celebrating its summer festival. Even as the planetary director is trying to settle some of the equipment squabbles, another of the screens in his office lights up, and the images of two self-conscious ten-year-old girls appear, inviting him to come to the festival.

"Today at twelve o'clock!" says the one in pink.

"At eleven!" says the one in blue.

"No, twelve!" pink insists.

"I'll be there!" the director shouts happily. "I'll definitely be there! And I'll be there at eleven and at twelve!" A special, joyful Russian exuberance.

But of course the director does not go to Children's Colony. Because this is the day that a new kind of wave appears, and none of the control devices have more than a trifling effect on it.

This time life on the entire planet will be wiped out—the innocent birds and the fish as well as the human beings. There will be a small number of exceptions. A few people will be able to escape on *Tariel*, the little supply ship that happens to be in port. It has a crew of three (Leonid Gorbovsky, captain; Mark Falkenstein, first officer; Percy Dixon, flight engineer) and is equipped to carry about ten passengers along with its cargo. By ruthless stripping, one might be able to crowd a hundred people aboard and still be able to fly. That will leave something over nine hundred to die on Rainbow—and the candidates include not only great physicists like

Etienne Lamondois and Alexandra Postysheva and the children (Alexandra has none, but Lamondois does) but also hapless tourists. Rainbow, though too far away for mass tourism, is popular both with artists and with honeymoon couples on account of its great beauty. At the moment the new wave form develops, there are about sixty visitors there.

Nor is it only people who have a claim to space on *Tariel*. There are scientists, quite prepared to die themselves, who are trying to get a few ounces of microfilm on board containing the results of thirty years of research. The great artist Johann Sourd happens to be on Rainbow; he hopes to get a single painting on board. And so on. Robert Sklyarov will do anything, literally anything, to get his Tanya aboard, though he expects to stay and die himself.

Obviously there are many symbolic levels here, including the level where we are hearing a nuclear parable. But it is as story that I love *Far Rainbow* best. There is such heroism on that last day. The Strugatskys describe it so movingly: the contrast between all that chicanery over who should get more equipment, and the terrible honesty as these same people confront death; the fifty or so perfect thumbnail sketches the Strugatskys draw; the final moment as the eight zero-pilots march, singing, into the sea, seven of them carrying the eighth who was blinded trying to jump the wave in a helicopter—well, there aren't many endings to a work of fiction that have so much in common with the end of a Beethoven symphony.

Owing to the blindness of publishers, you cannot at present buy *Far Rainbow*. But you can borrow it. Do.

Far Rainbow.
Arkady and Boris Strugatsky. 1964.

Epilogue
A Note on Availability

It would be merely tantalizing to write in praise of all these books without also giving some information on how to get hold of copies. So to end here's an alphabetized list of titles, reporting which ones are in print and giving editions and prices. Two warnings are in order. First, publishers tend to let books go in and out of print with great rapidity, and they are sometimes known to raise prices. Very soon after I complete the list it will begin to be inaccurate. But I think it will stay reasonably useful for some years.

Second, I have deliberately omitted one small group of reprints as being so overpriced that one has a sort of moral duty not to buy them. These are facsimile editions produced by any of several publishers who specialize in sales to libraries. A library committed to filling gaps in its collection is pretty much a captive market, and such publishers will cheerfully charge $60 or $80 for a book that (in my opinion) ought to cost maybe a third of that. They are, of course, free to charge what they please. I am equally free to leave them off this list.

As to the roughly dozen of these books not in print, all except two can be borrowed on interlibrary loan. Those two have never been published in the United States. They might form one part of an excuse to visit London.

Henry Adams. *Democracy: An American Novel*. Four editions are available. The three paperbacks are published by Airmont (n.d.), $1.50; Crown (1982), $4.95; and New American Library (1983), $3.50.

George Ade. *Fables in Slang*. Out of print in the U.S. Can be ordered from England. Dover (1960): paperback, £1.00.

The Adventures of Jonathan Corncob, Loyal American Refugee. Edited by Noel Perrin. David Godine (1976): hardcover, $8.95; paperback (1979), $7.95.

Diana Athill. *Instead of a Letter*. Carroll & Graf (1984): hardcover, $15.95; paperback, $7.95.

W. N. P. Barbellion. *The Journal of a Disappointed Man & A Last Diary*. Merrimack (1984): paperback, $8.95.

Peter S. Beagle. *A Fine and Private Place*. Ballantine (1976): paperback, $2.25.

The Best of Friends: Further Letters to Syndey Carlyle Cockerell. Edited by Viola Meynell. Never published in the U.S. Out of print in England.

Ernest Bramah. *Kai Lung's Golden Hours*. Out of print. Its companion volume, *The Wallet of Kai Lung* (nearly as funny) can be had in a hardcover edition from Buccaneer Books (1977) for $15.95.

Bryher. *Roman Wall*. Out of print.

James Branch Cabell. *The Silver Stallion*. Out of print in the U.S. Can be ordered from England. Unwin (1983): paperback, £2.95.

Jonathan Corncob. See *Adventures of Jonathan Corncob*.

James Gould Cozzens. *Guard of Honor*. Harcourt Brace Jovanovich, Harvest Books (1964): paperback, $8.95.

Syndey Carlyle Cockerell. See *Best of Friends*.

Walter de la Mare. *The Three Royal Monkeys*. Out of print.

The Diary of George Templeton Strong. Edited by Allan Nevins and Milton Thomas. Four vol. library reprint edition, $138. Abridged version, University of Washington Press (1988): paperback, $17.50; hardcover, $35.

Lord Dunsany. *The Blessing of Pan*. Out of print.

Emily Eden. *The Semi-Attached Couple*. Doubleday, Virago Modern Classics (1982): paperback, $8.95. (A bonus: the volume includes Miss Eden's other novel, *The Semi-Detached House*.)

Robert Graves. *Watch the North Wind Rise*. Farrar, Straus & Giroux (1949): paperback, $7.95.

Maureen Howard. *Bridgeport Bus*. Penguin (1980): paperback, $4.95.

William Dean Howells. *Indian Summer: A Novel.* Fromm International (1985): paperback, $8.95.

W. W. Jacobs. *Many Cargoes.* Ayer (1897 facsimile edition): $18. In addition, some of the stories are included in a slender volume called *Cargoes: Famous Stories of the Sea.* Branden (n.d.): paperback, $3.

Kenko. *Essays in Idleness: The Tsurezuregusa of Kenko.* Translated by Donald Keene. Columbia University Press (1967): paperback, $12.50.

Henry King. "The Exequy." The simplest place to find "The Exequy" is in *The Oxford Book of English Verse.*

Philip Larkin. "Church Going." In his volume *The Less Deceived,* which is out of print in the U.S. But the Marvell Press in England has an adequate paperback (hideous cover) for £3.60.

C. S. Lewis. *They Asked for a Paper.* Never published in the U.S. Most of the contents can be found in Lewis's *Selected Literary Essays,* edited by Walter Hooper. Cambridge University Press (1969): paperback, $13.95.

Rose Macaulay. *A Casual Commentary.* Ignoring one of those overpriced library reprint editions, out of print.

Michael Mathers. *Riding the Rails.* Out of print.

Hiram Maxim. *A Genius in the Family.* Dover (1936): paperback, $2.95.

Viola Meynell. See *Best of Friends.*

Joseph Mitchell. *The Bottom of the Harbor.* Out of print.

Eric Newby. *When the Snow Comes They Will Take You Away.* Washington Square Press (1984): paperback, $3.95.

Marcel Pagnol. *My Father's Glory* and *My Mother's House.* Translated by Rita Barisse. North Point Press (1986): hardcover, $20; paperback, $9.95.

Blanche C. Perrin. *Born to Race.* Out of print. (But it stayed in print for twenty-six years, which isn't bad.)

Gwen Raverat. *Period Piece.* A choice of two paperback editions. Faber & Faber (1960): $4.95; Norton (1976): $3.95.

Herbert Read. *The Green Child.* New Directions (1948): paperback, $5.95.

Henriette Roosenburg. *The Walls Came Tumbling Down.* Out of print.

Ernest Thompson Seton. *Wild Animals I Have Known.* Buccaneer (1986): hardcover, $18.95; Creative Arts (1987): paperback, $9.95; Penguin (1987): paperback, $7.95.

Freya Stark. *The Valleys of the Assassins*. Jeremy Tarcher (1983): hardcover, $9.95.

Stendhal. *On Love*. Translated by C. Scott Moncrieff. Da Capo (1983): paperback, $8.95. Under the title *Love*, translated by Gilbert and Suzanne Sale, Penguin (1975): paperback, $4.95; Merlin (1957): hardcover, $7.95.

George Templeton Strong. See *Diary of George Templeton Strong*.

Arkady and Boris Strugatsky. *Far Rainbow*. Out of print.

Daniele Varé. *The Maker of Heavenly Trousers*. Out of print in the U.S. Can be ordered from England. Black Swan (1986): paperback, £3.95.

Charles Williams. *All Hallows Eve*. Eerdmans (1981), paperback, $7.95.

Austin Tappan Wright. *Islandia*. Ayer (reprint of 1942 edition): hardcover, at the stiff but, for a twelve-hundred page book, bearable price of $40. New American Library: paperback, $12.95.